"The two most important days in your life are the day you are born and the day you find out why."

— Mark Twain

Imagine This

A quiet room where you can feel the tension in the air. People are moving around quickly, adjusting lights, checking the equipment to make sure everything is working properly, and a few staring intently at monitors, jotting down notes.

There's a large table in the middle of the room, filled with what looks like important tools, gadgets, and machines. At first glance, it feels like something serious is about to happen—maybe a life-saving operation.

The atmosphere is heavy, as if everyone is waiting for something big to occur. You can almost hear the clock ticking as the tension builds.

Suddenly, a person enters the room. He is wearing a white coat with a stethoscope around his neck, looking like a doctor or surgeon. The person walks confidently around the table, inspecting everything carefully. The room becomes even quieter as everyone watches, waiting for instructions.

The person takes a deep breath and says, "Is everything ready?" The team nods in agreement, and the air feels even more intense. The person walks around the table once more, making sure every detail is perfect. It seems like something important is about to start.

Then, the person suddenly breaks the tension with a grin. "Alright, let's do this! Lights, Camera, Medicine... sorry, Action!"

Wait, what's going on here? We thought this was some kind of important surgery.

Oh, it's not a surgery. It's actually a set from a corporate shoot! The intense atmosphere is just the pressure to get everything perfect for the brand.

And now, **what kind of director gives such commands?**

Well, maybe one who once dreamed of being a doctor. Or maybe a doctor who became a director.

Hi, I'm Raj—well, technically, Dr. Raj if you look at my education. But if you ask me, it's not the title that defines who I am. It's the journey that led me here, a journey that took me from being a doctor by education to a filmmaker by profession. It's a path that seemed set for me before I could even speak, but one I chose to rewrite.

So, here's my story. Not of how I became a doctor, but of how I became a filmmaker. And it all started with an entry into the world that was anything but ordinary.

Chapter 1:
Born Into the Operation Room

One fine day in 1994, I made my grand entrance into the world. Not as your typical, run-of-the-mill baby, but as the latest addition to a family of overachieving doctors. My father, a pediatrician, and my mother, a gynecologist, must have looked at me with that familiar, knowing look parents get when they realize their child is going to follow in their footsteps. "Ah, another doctor in the family," they probably thought. And let's face it, when your parents are both doctors, what else could you be but another one?

As a kid, I rarely saw my parents just sitting around at home, relaxing. Their lives were a whirlwind of hospital rounds, emergency calls, and late-night shifts. I'd be lying if I said I ever saw them sit down for a family dinner at a reasonable hour. Dinner was more like a race against time—one parent rushing off to an emergency while the other juggled paperwork between bites. While other kids had bedtime stories filled with dragons, princesses, and fairy tales, my lullabies were more like medical case studies. Instead of tales of mythical creatures, I grew up listening to stories about successful surgeries, miraculous recoveries, and the occasional heart-stopping moment where someone's life hung in the balance. No dragons, just dramatic medical procedures and life-or-death moments.

By the time I was able to walk, my toys weren't the usual trucks and action figures. No, I had plastic stethoscopes, syringes, and mini medical kits. My friends probably thought I was some sort of miniature healthcare professional in the making. My dolls had check-ups, and every now and then, I'd 'prescribe' something to my toys—just to practice, of course. I was practically playing doctor-doctor before I even knew what it really meant to be one.

By age six, I had already picked up enough medical terminology to leave most adults scratching their heads. I could probably name more diseases than the average person. Colds, flus, the occasional strep throat... if it had a name, I knew it. The dinner table conversations were always filled with debates on new treatments, medical breakthroughs, and the occasional friendly argument over which hospital had the best reputation. There were no debates about what I would become when I grew up—medicine was in my blood. It was practically our family's surname. The question wasn't *if* I would be a doctor; it was *which* branch of medicine I would specialize in.

My father, with that confident, parental pride, would lean back after a long day, look at me with a glint in his eye, and say, "One day, you'll be a great pediatrician, just like me." To me, it was as if he had already mapped out my future in medical charts. The thought of being anything other than a doctor seemed almost unimaginable.

I never had the luxury of deciding my future. Medicine was the only option that had been laid out for me, long before I could even understand what "profession" meant. It was assumed, not just expected, that I would follow this path. There was no "What do you want to be when you grow up?" question for me. I was simply told, "You will be a doctor." It was less of a question and more of a family tradition. A legacy passed down like a carefully curated heirloom.

Chapter 2:
The Boarding School Struggles

By the time I was in class 1, my parents decided to send me to a boarding school that was 100 kilometers away from home. Their reason? The best education, of course. It was all part of the grand plan to mold me into a well-rounded doctor. After all, what else would a six-year-old need to be good at besides science and medicine, right? But being sent off to boarding school at such a young age wasn't exactly my dream. I missed home, my bed, my parents, and—most importantly—the food. I would regularly cry myself to sleep, begging my parents to bring me back. But instead of coming to my rescue, they just... changed my hostel. And not just any change—this new hostel was 500 kilometers away.

Yes, you heard that right. From 100 kilometers to 500. As if that would somehow make things better. But they were convinced it would give me a more "mature" experience. And so, I spent the next eight years of my life there, with its fair share of ups and downs.

But here's the thing: I wasn't just any kid. I was the plumpy kid. At the age of 13, I was already tipping the scales at around 100 kilograms. When I arrived at my new hostel, I was already the "big guy" on the block. On the very first day, they served Maggi for dinner, and I started eating like I hadn't seen food in years. I ate not one but two big bowls of Maggi. And that, of course, was when my classmates got their first "entertainment" of the year. They laughed and pointed at me as if I was some kind of circus act.

But that was just the beginning. It wasn't just about being plump; I became an easy target for bullying. My seniors—kids who were a few years older than me—would constantly make fun of me. They would mock my size and weight, grab my chest, squeezing it in a way as if they were handling a woman's breasts, and make cruel jokes about how I looked "more like a girl than a boy." They'd laugh, asking if I needed a bra, which made me feel pathetic.

Every day, I had to deal with this kind of humiliation. Whether I was in class, walking in the hallway, or just sitting with my lunch, there they were, making fun of me. It was like I had become their favorite target. They would make cruel jokes, say things to embarrass me, and I would just stand there, feeling small and powerless. I didn't know how to defend myself. I was too young and scared to say anything back.

Every time they did that, I felt like I was less of a person. Every insult hit deep, tearing away my confidence bit by bit. Their laughter was the worst—it wasn't just laughter; it was a constant reminder that they saw me as an object of ridicule, someone they could humiliate without a second thought. I used to cry every day, feeling so helpless and ashamed of my body. Each time they did it, I would freeze. I didn't know how to respond. I was just 13 or 14, while they were 16 or 17—older, bigger, and more confident. I didn't stand a chance.

One day, a senior came up to me and asked me to remove my clothes and masturbate in front of them. I didn't even know what that meant back then, but I could sense it wasn't something good. When I refused to do what he asked, he started beating me—hitting me like I was nothing more than an animal. And no, that wasn't the last time. It became a regular thing. Every month, someone or the other would beat me, just because I didn't do what they wanted, as if I was their slave. They'd beat me with whatever was closest—bed supports, metal rods from the curtains, anything they could get their hands on. It didn't matter if I was tired or if I was scared. If I didn't obey the master, the beating would follow. After every beating, they'd laugh and proudly discuss who'd done the "best job," like it was some kind of achievement.

The pain, both physical and emotional, felt like it would never stop. There were so many nights when I felt like I didn't want to live anymore. I thought about jumping off the roof to end it all, to make the pain go away. But every time I thought about it, something stopped me—not fear of dying, but fear of failing and waking up to even worse punishment.

Every year, I would go to my father and beg him to change my boarding school. I would tell him how miserable my life was, how my seniors bully me, and how I just wanted to be at home. Every year, he would ask, "Tell me who is bullying you and what are they doing?" and then he would say to manage things on my own. "Papa, how do you expect me to tell you that these narcissistic guys here love to sexually abuse me by touching my chest, ask me to remove my clothes, and force me to masturbate in front of them? And if I don't obey, they beat me up like an animal. How am I supposed to stand up to guys who are twice my size, who look like they could bench press a small car?"

But instead of changing my school, he gave me a pep talk and sent me back to face another year of misery. He genuinely believed that a few words of encouragement could somehow make everything better—like the endless teasing, the cruel taunting, and the pain could just vanish. But those faces—the ones of the people who bullied me—still haunt me, spinning in my mind, forever.

By class 8, life in boarding school became routine. I'd grown used to feeling homesick, dealing with the bullying, and surviving on my own. Then, something new happened—our school built a squash court. It was pristine, with polished walls and a brand-new floor.

Now, squash wasn't as popular as cricket or football. Most kids stuck to the usual games, and since I wasn't exactly a star player in any of them, I rarely got picked for teams. Being the plump kid meant I was always the last choice. Whether it was cricket or basketball, no one wanted me slowing them down. Honestly, I can't blame them. Running across the field felt like running a marathon, and let's just say, stamina wasn't my strong suit.

But squash was different. Hardly anyone used the court, so I decided to give it a try. Here's the catch, though—squash is a two-player game. But since no one ever volunteered to play with me, I played alone. I'd hit the ball against the wall, watch it bounce back, and hit it again. It became my thing. Just me, the ball, and the wall.

Day after day, I kept playing. At first, it was just for fun, but slowly, I noticed something. My clothes started feeling loose, and the chubby cheeks I'd carried around for years began to slim down. By the end of the year, I'd lost 20 to 30 kilograms. The transformation was unreal.

Suddenly, I wasn't just the "fat kid" anymore. My confidence grew, and even though the bullying didn't completely stop, I felt stronger, both physically and mentally. Squash had given me something no other sport ever did—a sense of accomplishment.

Chapter 3: The Math Lover in a Biologist's World

I have to admit, books and I always had a complicated relationship. Most of them could put me to sleep in minutes—even those novels my friends loved to read. For me, opening a book was like taking a sleeping pill. Math was the one exception, the only subject that actually kept me awake. It felt more like solving puzzles than studying, so I didn't mind spending time on it.

Every other subject, though, was a struggle. Take geography, for example. One day, my teacher asked me where red soil is found in India. I had no clue. She gave me two tight slaps right there for not knowing, but honestly, I still don't know where it's found. And, to be fair, I don't think knowing that would've made any difference in my life.

Then, as if by miracle, came Facebook. When I was in 10th grade, it became this massive trend. Everyone was on it, and I decided to join too. One day, I found a girl from my hometown on there, someone I had always liked but never had the guts to talk to. We knew each other from childhood, but I never really got the chance to speak to her in person. I sent her a message, and to my surprise, she responded. What started as a simple "Hi" turned into hours of conversation. We talked about everything, from school to hobbies to silly things that made us laugh. It felt like we could talk forever.

We kept chatting for months, maybe even years. Every conversation felt easy, and we shared so many moments of laughter and connection. I really liked her, but every time I thought about telling her how I felt, I would freeze. The fear of rejection was too strong, and I couldn't gather the courage to confess. Even though we had so many great conversations, I kept those feelings hidden, afraid that things might change if I told her the truth. We just stayed friends, talking for hours, but I never told her how much I actually liked her.

Then came class 11. While most kids at school were busy figuring out what they liked, I had my love story sorted early: Mathematics. I absolutely adored solving equations, cracking puzzles, and playing with numbers—it was my idea of fun. I could sit for hours with my notebook, finding joy in every solution I worked out.

But, of course, life had other plans—or rather, my parents did. When I reached class 11, they "suggested" I take up biology. By "suggested," I mean I was left with no choice. The dream of me becoming a doctor was still alive and kicking in their minds. But since I couldn't let go of my beloved math, I ended up taking the combo: Math with Biology. Yep, I signed myself up for double the torture. On one hand, I had biology, with its endless diagrams and technical terms. On the other, I had math, which felt like a breath of fresh air in an otherwise suffocating schedule.

Deep down, I wanted to be an engineer. I dreamed of building things, solving real-world problems, and doing something that truly excited me. Engineering seemed like the perfect path for someone who loved math as much as I did. But here I was, stuck with mitochondria, stomata, and xylem. Trust me, if there was a poll for the world's most boring subject, I'd vote for biology every day.

Then came class 12, the big one. The year that decides your future—or at least that's what every child is told. Honestly, I wasn't exactly the most studious kid around. While some kids were glued to their books, I was more of a "let's get through this" kind of student.

Biology, though, was my nemesis. No matter how much I tried, I just couldn't wrap my head around it. The diagrams, the endless names, and all those life processes—it was like trying to learn an alien language. My biggest fear was that biology would drag down my overall percentage. So, I did what any terrified student would do: I spent the entire year memorizing biology. Every spare minute was devoted to reading and re-reading those hefty textbooks.

One saving grace, however, was chemistry, all thanks to my teacher, Leena Ma'am. She had this incredible way of simplifying even the toughest concepts, making chemistry feel almost effortless. Her teaching gave me such a solid grasp of the subject that, even in a year as hectic as class 12, chemistry never felt like a struggle.

With biology taking up most of my time and energy, I completely neglected my first love—Math.

It didn't hit me until 15 days before the board exams. I had a sudden realization: "I haven't studied a single chapter of maths!" Panic set in. If I didn't do something fast, I'd flunk for sure. So, I rolled up my sleeves and did the impossible—I crammed an entire year's worth of math in just 15 days.

For two weeks straight, I breathed, ate, and slept math. Every formula, every theorem, every exercise—I went through it all. And when the board exam finally arrived, I walked in with nothing but sheer determination.

The days after math exams were a blur of other subjects. Chemistry, physics, and the dreaded biology—all required their own focus, but by now, I was so mentally drained that I could barely keep track of the time. Every exam felt like another hurdle, but with each passing day, I knew I was closer to being free. The last paper came, and with it, the feeling that the pressure was finally over.

Now that the boards were over, I felt relieved to finally leave that place that had felt like a prison for so long. Eight years of bullying had been tough. While most people were sad about leaving their school, I was happy because I knew I wouldn't be bullied anymore. I remember thinking, *Life can't get worse than this—wherever I go next, it has to be better.* The thought of never going back to that school felt like a huge weight was lifted off my shoulders.

A month later, the results came. I opened my marksheet, and my eyes scanned the numbers. I had scored 99 out of 100 in math, despite only having 15 days of prep. Chemistry wasn't far behind, with another 99, thanks to Leena Ma'am's exceptional teaching. My overall percentage? A solid 93%. It was the best I'd ever done. To give you some perspective, I'd never scored more than 85% before, thanks to my old foes: biology and, of course, English.

But this time, I didn't just pass. I topped my entire district. The boy who struggled with his weight, got bullied, and dreaded biology had managed to beat the odds and emerge as the top scorer.

Chapter 4: The Struggle Between Dreams and Expectations

After topping my district, I thought I had achieved everything. It felt like I had reached the highest point of success—at least, that's what I believed at the time. I thought of myself as someone who had done what no one else could, someone who should be celebrated. My achievement felt huge, like I had finally earned my place in the world. It was an exciting feeling, the kind that made me feel unstoppable. But once the excitement faded, I started to wonder, "What's next?" And that's when everything began to go wrong.

I had always wanted to pursue engineering, but my dad had different plans. He was determined that I should follow in his footsteps and become a doctor. He would often say, "Beta, ek baar MBBS kar lo, phir toh aish hi aish hai (just complete your MBBS once, and then life will be all fun and comfort)," painting it as the ultimate path to success and stability. According to him, engineering wasn't the same—he believed engineers didn't earn well and would bring up examples of relatives who had completed engineering but were still jobless. I tried explaining that biology wasn't my passion and that engineering was where I felt I truly belonged, but instead of understanding, our conversation turned into a huge argument.

My dad, being a doctor, couldn't understand why I didn't want the same career. To him, becoming a doctor seemed like the only sensible choice. He thought it would provide me stability and respect—values he had grown up with. But I didn't want to spend my life surrounded by biology books and hospitals. I wanted to design, build, and create things, not diagnose and treat people.

We argued for days. I couldn't understand why he couldn't see things from my point of view. After all, I had topped my district. Shouldn't that be enough? But no, my dreams were being pushed aside for his expectations. We stopped talking for a month.

Things didn't get better until my mom stepped in. She realized that both of us were too stubborn. After many discussions, it was decided that I would try preparing for the MBBS entrance exam for a year. If I didn't like it, I could switch to engineering afterward. To help me get ready, they sent me for a three-month crash course in medical entrance preparation.

However, the crash course didn't help much. In fact, it made things worse. I felt lost. Biology was a struggle, and I couldn't understand the concepts. Physics seemed way too complicated, and no matter how many times I tried, I just couldn't get it. The only subject that felt okay was chemistry, thanks to my school teacher, Leena Ma'am, who had explained chemistry clearly in school. She was the only reason I felt somewhat confident during the course.

But even that small comfort couldn't keep me going. The three months were filled with frustration, confusion, and a growing sense of failure. I had two major mental breakdowns, crying on the phone to my parents, begging them to let me quit and follow my dream of becoming an engineer. It felt like no one understood how unhappy I was, how much I was struggling. I felt like my dreams were slipping further away every day.

Finally, the three months ended, and it was time to take the MBBS entrance exam. I knew deep down that I wasn't prepared enough, but I had no other choice. I gave it my best, even though my heart wasn't in it. And, as expected, I got a low rank, which meant I wouldn't be able to get into a good medical college. The only option left was to join a private medical college.

Chapter 5: The Race to Medical School

After getting a low rank in my first MBBS entrance, my parents suggested I take another year to prepare. I reminded them of the earlier talk about "trying engineering if I didn't like medicine," but now, they were asking me to "just give it one more try." Honestly, I didn't have many options—I wasn't earning, and they were the ones funding my studies, so I had no other choice but to agree.

I joined a new coaching institute. This place was huge, with around 2,000 students in that branches. In my batch, we had around 40 students, but despite the relatively smaller number, the competition felt intense. The other students seemed so much more focused and dedicated, and it was clear that many of them had been preparing for longer than I had. Until then, I thought my 93% in school was impressive, but now I was surrounded by an army of equally high-scoring students.

On the very first day, we had an orientation session, which was supposed to give us a preview of what the coming months would be like. The botany teacher wasted no time in delivering a reality check. "Every year, around 5 lakh students appear for the MBBS entrance," he told us. "Out of those, only 3,000 make it to government medical seats. So, at most, one or two people from this batch will actually secure a seat." His words hit hard, and I couldn't help but look around the room at my peers. Everyone seemed so determined, and in that moment, I thought, "If only one or two people make it, I don't think it'll be me."

There was one student who stood out among the others. He was the epitome of a dedicated, textbook-perfect student. You could tell he had studied every book, knew every detail, and had the discipline to back it up. If anyone from our batch was going to make it, it would be him, no doubt about it.

As the classes progressed, I stuck with it, even though biology, in particular, was a constant struggle for me. Thankfully, our physics teacher was great, and he managed to clear up a lot of confusion I had with the subject. The concepts started to make sense, and I began to feel more confident in my understanding. Physics, which had once seemed so difficult, was now a subject I could at least manage.

However, biology remained a different beast altogether. The teachers insisted that the entire MBBS exam paper would be based solely on the NCERT textbooks. This sounded simple enough, but I just couldn't wrap my head around the subject. The complexity of the topics, the names, and processes were overwhelming. I realized that understanding biology in depth was probably out of my reach, at least for now. So, I had no choice but to fall back on cramming the entire book. I started memorizing the 100-120 pages of the NCERT textbook, hoping that if I repeated the information enough times, it would stick.

The process was grueling. There was no logic to it, just sheer repetition. I would go over terms like "photosynthesis" and "mitosis" over and over again, hoping I could recall them when the time came. I didn't understand the mechanics behind the words, but I knew I had to memorize them. It was a strategy of survival rather than learning. And for me, at that point, survival was all that mattered.

But as months went by, those high-achieving students around me started getting distracted. They were busy with new girlfriends, talking on the phone for hours, bringing gifts, or bunking classes. Soon, only about 15-20 of us were regularly attending sessions, and I kept pushing myself.

Chapter 6:
Pushing Through the Grind

The months dragged on, and with each passing day, the pressure mounted. Every hour seemed consumed by lectures, study sessions, and the constant pressure to do more. I could feel myself slipping into a routine of stress and exhaustion. Every day felt like I was running a race I wasn't sure I could finish. The competition around me seemed fierce, and I was constantly comparing myself to my peers, many of whom appeared far more focused and prepared.

But beyond the lectures and study sessions, something unexpected became a lifeline for me: running.

Growing up, I had always struggled with my weight. In school, I managed to stay somewhat in control by playing squash—a sport I enjoyed and that kept me active. But when I moved for coaching in preparation for the MBBS entrance, I was faced with a new challenge: there was no squash court nearby, and I needed a way to maintain my fitness. I had always been a plump kid, and I knew that if I didn't stay on top of my weight, I'd start feeling even worse about myself.

So, I decided to give running a try. I started waking up early, before the sun had risen, and I would head out for a run. The first few days were brutal. My body wasn't used to the strain, and every step felt like a struggle. The soreness in my legs was almost unbearable, and I found myself questioning if this was really worth it. But as I pushed through those early mornings, something slowly began to change.

Running became my escape. It wasn't just about fitness—it was about finding a way to breathe and clear my mind. The first few minutes of every run were the hardest. My body felt heavy, and my mind was filled with the overwhelming thoughts of my studies. But once I found my rhythm, everything else seemed to fade away. The constant pressure, the long hours of studying, and the stress of competition all took a backseat to the rhythm of my footsteps.

As the days passed, my runs became longer and more consistent. What started as a simple way to stay in shape transformed into something far more important. I began running 8-10 kilometers a day, no matter what. Whether the temperature was scorching hot or the rain was pouring down, I made sure to wake up and run. It wasn't just about maintaining my weight anymore; it became an integral part of my routine that I couldn't skip. No matter how tired I was from studying or how tough the day ahead seemed, I always made time for that run.

As I kept running, I started noticing changes in my body. The weight I had worked so hard to keep under control was dropping faster than I anticipated. There came a time when I looked in the mirror and didn't recognize the person staring back at me. My mom, noticed it too. She told me, "You're starting to look underweight!"

It was a strange feeling—the same guy who had once weighed 100 kilograms and felt self-conscious about his plump physique was now looking underweight.

Chapter 7:
The Test of Persistence

So, by the time the entrance exam started getting closer, the coaching began holding monthly tests with around 10,000 students across different branches. My first test didn't go great—I ranked around 3,000 out of 10,000, which was not where I wanted to be. But I kept pushing myself. Gradually, my ranks started improving. By the 3rd or 4th monthly test, I was getting around the 1,000-2,000 rank range—not amazing, but a definite improvement.

A month before the entrance, our coaching completed the course, and we were given study leave to revise. Physics and chemistry felt manageable, but biology was still my nightmare. I spent almost 8-10 hours every day trying to memorize the NCERT pages. I would cram, forget, then cram again. The process gave me massive headaches. I remember thinking, "Who came up with these names—mitochondria, plasmodesmata? If I ever meet the person, I'll give them a piece of my mind."

Finally, the day of the entrance arrived. When I reached the center, I saw thousands of students intensely revising their notes. I just had my admit card and a pen, feeling more nervous about forgetting what I'd crammed than anything else. Standing outside the exam center, I watched other students frantically flipping through their notes. Some were pacing up and down, mouthing formulas to themselves. Me? I just had my admit card and a pen. I hadn't even brought my books—there was no way I'd manage to cram anything more into my head.

The exam itself was a blur. I answered the questions as best as I could, trying not to overthink every little thing. Once it was over, I walked out feeling a strange mix of relief and dread. My preparation hadn't been perfect, but the thought of one more day cramming biology terms was just... unbearable. I didn't know what to expect, but part of me had already braced for disappointment.

Then came the AIIMS entrance, just fifteen days after the MBBS test. AIIMS was the ultimate dream for anyone in medical prep. Still riding on my exam high, I thought, why not give it a shot? So, with the last bits of energy I had left, I went in for round two.

After that, I was done. I went home, closed my books, and actually started enjoying life for a change. Results were weeks away, and honestly, I wasn't expecting much.

But when that day arrived, I felt the nerves all over again. When I checked my MBBS entrance result, I couldn't believe my eyes: All India Rank **615**. Out of 5 lakh students! I was in a daze, reading the screen over and over. Was this real? Was I actually going to get a government medical seat? In that moment, I felt like I'd climbed a mountain.

The thrill of that rank felt like being back on the high I'd experienced when I scored 93% in school. There was that same rush, the same feeling of doing something people didn't quite expect from me. In school, that score had earned me a reputation as a "bright student," and now, this rank felt like a continuation of that success story. It wasn't just about the number—it was the realization that all those hours and the endless grind had finally paid off, and that I'd actually achieved something I hadn't fully dared to expect.

But there was still one more surprise waiting. Fifteen days later, the AIIMS results came in, and there it was: Rank **635**. I'd not only made it to a medical college—I'd made it to AIIMS. I was going to study with some of the top students in the country.

Suddenly, the high I'd felt with the MBBS rank shot into an altogether different zone. Making it into AIIMS felt surreal, like I'd hit the peak. In that moment, it felt like no one could be better than me. I'd not only cracked one of the toughest exams in the country but had made it to the most prestigious medical institute, which I thought was nearly out of reach for someone like me. It was like an almost unbeatable victory—a feeling that, for that day at least, I was at the top.

As for that nerdy guy in my batch, the one who seemed like the sure shot? Unluckily, he wasn't able to secure a good rank.

Chapter 8: A New Beginning

After I was selected for AIIMS, I was allotted AIIMS Patna in the first round of counseling. I was excited but also nervous. Ragging in Indian medical colleges has a bad reputation, and after everything I had gone through in school, I was scared it would be the same. The thought of facing more bullying, especially from seniors, made me anxious. As the day to leave for Patna drew closer, I couldn't stop thinking about what might happen. What if my seniors were like the ones I had to deal with in school? What if I had to go through more humiliation? These thoughts kept troubling me as I packed my bags.

Finally, the day arrived, and I reported to AIIMS Patna. I met my batchmates, and we all felt a mix of excitement and nervousness. Our campus had only opened a year ago, so we were just the second batch to join. The first batch had only 50 students, while our batch had 100. The college was still new, and it gave off a fresh vibe, which made me feel a little better. But, even with that, I couldn't stop worrying about ragging. I wondered if things would get worse and if I would have to deal with difficult seniors again.

As days passed, though, things weren't as bad as I had feared. Most of our seniors were kind and helpful. They understood we were new and needed guidance, so they would answer questions, help us with the campus, and generally made us feel comfortable. There were a few seniors who tried to be tough and would ask for our names in a gruff way or give us a sharp look. But even these seniors weren't as bad as I imagined. They didn't try to hurt us or make us feel small. Instead, they became our friends over time, and it wasn't long before the whole batch was like a big family.

I was relieved that the ragging was not as intense as I had heard. It wasn't perfect, but I could see that most of my seniors had good intentions. They were here to help us succeed, not to bring us down. This was such a huge change from my past experiences. For the first time in years, I felt like I was in a place where I could focus on what mattered the most—my studies and my future.

I felt thankful that things were so different here. I had feared the worst, but I found a supportive environment where I could learn and grow without the fear of bullying or ragging. AIIMS Patna gave me a fresh start, and with that, I could finally look forward to what was to come.

Chapter 9:
In the Army of Toppers

When our classes at AIIMS Patna began, I firmly believed I would continue to be the top student. After all, I had been the batch topper in my coaching institute. With that confidence, I walked into the lecture hall on day one, armed with 10 different-colored pens—each one for a different task—and took my seat at the front. It was a habit I had carried over from coaching, where I fought to sit in the front row to be closest to the teacher. I was determined to do the same here at AIIMS. I copied down every word the professors spoke and every diagram they drew. This continued for the first three months. I thought I had everything figured out. I was going to be the best doctor India had ever seen. I believed that all I needed to do was keep cramming and memorizing, and it would all fall into place.

However, I soon realized that things weren't as simple as they had been in coaching. The difference in the syllabus was massive. In coaching, I could manage to memorize around 100 to 120 pages of notes, and that was enough to top the batch. But here, the textbooks were not only thick, but also filled with thousands of pages, and each subject demanded multiple books. I was used to cramming, so I continued with the same approach—writing down everything, memorizing as much as I could, sometimes even to the point of exhaustion. I didn't understand much of biology, and in medical school, where biology is the backbone of everything, I struggled even more. But I thought I could overcome that by sheer willpower and memorization. The pressure to be the best, to be the top scorer, pushed me further into this habit of cramming. My head would ache from all the memorization, but I continued because I was determined to succeed. I was living in a bubble of my own making, thinking that if I just kept pushing myself, I would eventually succeed.

Then came the first semester exams. With the same old confidence, I walked into the exam hall, certain that my cramming would pay off. I had memorized everything, or at least I thought I had. I sat down at my desk, organized my pens, and looked around at my classmates. They all seemed focused. Then the exam started, and I dove straight in. Each question felt important, like a test of my abilities and my future. I wrote as fast as I could, trying to remember everything I had studied. Some questions were easy, but others were difficult—things I hadn't expected. Still, I kept writing, hoping my effort would be enough.

Finally, the results were posted. I stood in front of the notice board, my heart racing. I scanned the list, looking for my name, but when I found it, I couldn't believe what I saw. I had barely passed and was among the bottom 20 students. I felt like the ground had been pulled out from under me. I had worked so hard, but it wasn't enough.

I couldn't understand how this had happened. I had studied non-stop. I had believed that all my effort would pay off, but it didn't. That's when I realized—I wasn't the only one who had been a topper. Everyone in my batch had been a topper in their own coaching institutes. I was in the middle of an army of toppers—each one as determined and driven as I was. I wasn't unique anymore. I wasn't the only one who had worked hard. In fact, I was just one of many.

Soon, I realized: the medical curriculum was nothing like what I had experienced in coaching. In coaching, the syllabus was focused, and the books were short. But here, the textbooks were thousands of pages long, and there were so many subjects to cover. Cramming everything was impossible.

That was when I realized that cramming wouldn't work here. The medical syllabus was vast, the textbooks thick, and the competition fierce. I couldn't just memorize and expect to pass. But instead of changing my approach, I did the exact opposite: I stopped trying altogether.

Biology, the core of medical studies, had always been a struggle for me, and now, it felt impossible. No matter how much I crammed, it was clear that I couldn't understand it. The pressure of keeping up with the constant flow of information, combined with the realization that memorizing everything was simply not feasible, made me give up. I couldn't see a way forward, and instead of facing the challenge, I shut down.

I started showing up to class empty-handed, just attending those classes to maintain my attendance. I no longer had the energy to fight for the front seat or keep up with every detail in the textbooks. The boy who used to fight for the first bench with 10 pens now found himself fighting for the last bench. I stopped taking notes and stopped paying attention. I had no pens in hand, no books open—I was there just to sleep through the lectures. I had gone from the eager student who once wanted to be the best to someone who just wanted to get through the day.

The boy who once wanted to be the best doctor India ever had now just wanted to make it through each day. The dream had faded, replaced by confusion, exhaustion, and a sense of helplessness.

Chapter 10:
The Distraction of Freedom

As I entered my second semester at AIIMS, my enthusiasm for studying began to fade. I was no longer the focused student who had once believed that hard work and discipline would carry me through. Slowly but surely, I stopped studying altogether. The relentless pressure of trying to be the best started to take its toll, and my once-structured routine collapsed. Instead of immersing myself in textbooks, I found solace in something else: the free Wi-

Fi that was available on campus. It was like a hidden treasure I could access any time, and I took full advantage of it.

The Wi-Fi became my new obsession. Instead of spending my nights studying or preparing for exams, I spent hours streaming movies, binge-watching YouTube videos, and occasionally diving into the depths of the internet for things I shouldn't have been looking at. I was so engrossed in this new routine that studying seemed like a distant memory. The internet had become my escape, my distraction from the overwhelming pressure of medical school.

I would find myself sitting in the campus corridor at night, hunched over my phone, downloading movies, shows, and whatever else caught my interest. I wasn't interested in what was happening in class. I had stopped caring about my textbooks, my notes, and even the lectures. It wasn't that I didn't want to succeed anymore; I just couldn't handle the weight of trying to be perfect all the time. So, I turned to something easier, something that didn't require me to think too much.

This is when I met Ajay. We started spending more time together, and soon we became inseparable. He was the kind of person who could always find a way to make things fun, even when everything else seemed dull. We'd wander around campus, hang out in the malls, or simply enjoy each other's company. Ajay was my escape from the loneliness I had begun to feel in this new place. It was through him that I realized there was more to life than just studying.

I was in a co-ed environment now, and for the first time, I was surrounded by girls of my age. It was an experience I wasn't used to, coming from a boys' school where conversations about relationships and dating were pretty much nonexistent.

I started to notice how my friends from school would talk about their girlfriends. It was something I had never really understood before, but now I couldn't help but feel like I was missing out. I wasn't the kind of person who had relationships in school, and now I saw all these people with partners, and I couldn't shake the feeling that I needed a girlfriend too.

There were around 35-40 girls in my batch, and naturally, some of them caught my eye. I found myself attracted to a few of them, and before long, I realized that most of them were active on Facebook. It seemed like the perfect opportunity, so I sent friend requests to a few of the girls I found interesting. To my surprise, many of them accepted, and before I knew it, I was chatting with one of them regularly.

She was beautiful, and our conversations flowed effortlessly. We would talk for hours, and for the first time in a long while, I felt like I was connecting with someone. She was funny, smart, and easy to talk to. It felt like a breath of fresh air, a welcome distraction from the pressure of medical school. The conversations slowly became a highlight of my day, and I looked forward to them every time I logged onto Facebook.

But during all this, the girl from my school, the one I had mentioned before, tried to reach out to me again. I had nearly forgotten about her, buried in my new life at AIIMS, but here she was, trying to rekindle our old friendship. She texted me, and at first, I was caught off guard. I wasn't sure how to respond. But by then, I was too distracted by my growing connection with the girl from my batch. Maybe I was being a fool, ignoring someone who had once meant so much to me. But I was swept up in the whirlwind of this new experience, and I chose to focus on what was right in front of me.

Months passed, and I continued to chat with the girl from my batch. I started developing feelings for her, and after months of conversation, I finally decided to take the leap. February 8th, Propose Day, seemed like the perfect opportunity. I gathered all my courage and proposed to her. I had built up this moment in my head for so long, thinking that it was going to be the beginning of something special.

When she responded, it wasn't at all what I had expected. Her words were vague, unclear, almost like she was avoiding giving me a direct answer. She didn't say yes, but she didn't exactly say no either. It was a response that left me hanging, unsure of what she truly felt, but in my gut, I knew. It was one of those moments where you don't need the final, crushing "no" to understand that the answer is clear: she wasn't interested in me the same way.

It felt like a punch to the stomach. My mind tried to make sense of it, but my heart was already breaking. There was no straight-up rejection, no cold, hard "I'm not interested," but there didn't need to be. The vagueness of her answer said it all. And I understood immediately.

As I read her response over and over again, I felt this heavy weight in my chest. It wasn't just disappointment; it was a deep, almost suffocating sense of self-doubt. *Am I not good enough? What did I do wrong?* The questions kept spiraling in my head, and for the first time in a long time, I was hit with a feeling of deep disappointment in myself. I had tried so hard, put myself out there, and yet, it didn't matter. It wasn't enough.

It was gut-wrenching, to say the least. It wasn't just the rejection—it was the feeling of not being seen or appreciated the way I had imagined. In that moment, I felt like all the things I thought I was good at didn't matter. My heart felt hollow, like it was carrying the weight of that unspoken rejection.

I tried to brush it off, tell myself it wasn't a big deal, but deep down, I knew it hurt. And it hurt more than I was willing to admit.

Chapter 11: The First Sip

I was feeling completely crushed after the rejection, and Ajay could see it. He was always the kind of friend who wanted to help, even if he didn't know exactly how. "Have a drink, man. It'll make you feel better," he suggested, trying to cheer me up. He could see how upset I was, and I guess he thought that a little alcohol might help take the edge off.

Now, anyone who knew me knew I was a teetotaler. I had never been into alcohol. It just wasn't my thing, and to be honest, I didn't understand why people drank. I'd always stayed away from it and never saw the point. But Ajay wasn't the type of friend to just let me be. He wasn't going to give up on me that easily.

Seeing me so down, he took me to another friend's room, Apoorv's. Apoorv was another one of our friends, and he always seemed to have a calm vibe. When we got there, he handed me a bottle of beer. "Just try it," he said, like it was no big deal.

I hesitated. I didn't want to drink. I didn't want to start now, but I was so exhausted emotionally, and the pain from the rejection was still eating away at me. I was looking for something, anything, to make me feel better. Maybe this would help, I thought, even though deep down I knew it wouldn't. But Ajay and Apoorv were persistent, and I felt like I needed to try something, so I finally gave in.

I opened the bottle and took a sip.

The moment it hit my tongue, I realized just how wrong I was to think it might help. The taste was awful—bitter and sharp, like I had just swallowed something that didn't belong in my mouth. Yuck! I immediately regretted it. The taste stayed with me, a weird aftertaste that I couldn't shake off. It was nothing like I imagined. I'd always heard people talk about alcohol like it was some kind of special experience, but I didn't understand it. How could people like this? How could they get addicted to this taste?

I started questioning myself, wondering, *How do people actually enjoy this stuff?* It made no sense to me. I had always thought alcohol was supposed to make you feel better, but instead, it just made me feel worse. It didn't numb the pain at all. If anything, it just made me feel emptier, like I was trying to cover up my sadness with something that didn't work.

So there I was, sitting with my friends, holding a bottle that promised comfort but gave me nothing but a bitter taste. It was a moment of clarity. I understood that no matter how many times I tried to drown my feelings, they would still be there. The alcohol wasn't going to help me. I needed to face what I was feeling, no matter how painful it was.

Chapter 12:
The Freedom of Pedals

After the heartbreak, I found myself at a complete standstill, stuck in a strange state of limbo. Days passed with me glued to YouTube, watching random videos all day—anything that could help me pass the time and distract me from reality.

Then came the first-year exams, which somehow I managed to pass—let's just say I found ways to get by. It was one of those situations where I relied more on luck and a bit of "help" here and there.

Every now and then, I'd catch myself wondering about my future, asking, *What am I even doing with my life?*

Deep down, I knew that medicine wasn't something I could stick with. It felt like I was walking a path that wasn't my own, following a script that had been handed to me rather than one I truly wanted to read. So, I started daydreaming, imagining myself doing other things. Some days, I'd think about doing an MBA and working in a big corporate office, wearing suits, giving presentations, the whole deal. Other days, the idea of preparing for the civil services would pop into my head, and I'd picture myself as an officer with power and respect. But none of these dreams seemed real; they were more like quick escapes, like flipping through random channels without truly watching anything. I was lost, and I knew it.

Amidst all of this, one day, a friend suggested I buy a bicycle so we could ride to the market. I thought it was a good idea, so I asked my father for one. He understood that I needed some physical activity to stay fit, and buying me a bicycle seemed like a good way to keep me active. So, he got me one.

What I thought would be a way to just get to the market turned into something much bigger.

After I got the bicycle, I started riding it every day. I would go for a ride after my lectures, and it quickly became my favorite part of the day. I would ride for 20-30 km, just going wherever I felt like. There was something special about being on the bike. It gave me a sense of freedom. Pedaling away, feeling the breeze on my face, made me forget about everything else.

One day, during a holiday, I decided to take my bike out early in the morning. I had no plan, just the urge to ride. I kept going, and soon I found myself in a place I didn't recognize. I had no idea how to get back, but I didn't panic. I just kept pedaling, thinking I would figure it out eventually. That day, I ended up riding for about 12-14 hours, covering almost 100 km. By the time I got back to my campus, I was tired, but I felt good.

Chapter 13: A New Obsession

Then our junior batch arrived, and that's when things took an unexpected turn. There was this junior named Junaid. He was a friendly guy, but more than that, he had something I'd been secretly fascinated with for years—a DSLR camera. Ever since I was a kid, I'd been drawn to cameras, especially those with big lenses. I'd always wondered how it would feel to hold one, to snap a photo with that satisfying click. But it was the kind of thing that felt out of reach, almost like a luxury that wasn't meant for me.

Normally, I wouldn't even think about borrowing anything from anyone, but this time was different. One day, after gathering some courage, I went up to junaid and asked, "junaid, do you mind if I borrow your camera for a day or two?" To my surprise, junaid agreed without hesitation. He handed it over as if he was lending a pen, not a prized piece of gear. I could hardly believe my luck.

The moment I held that camera, something shifted inside me. I felt an instant connection, like this was what I had been searching for all along. I started experimenting with it right away, taking photos of everything around me—trees, benches, people passing by. Every click of the shutter felt incredibly satisfying. It was like seeing the world through a different lens, literally and metaphorically. I could feel the thrill of capturing little moments, freezing them in time with just one click. It felt almost magical.

During those days, I didn't let the camera out of my sight. At night, I'd even keep it on the bed beside me, like it was something precious, something I couldn't bear to part with. I was completely hooked. I'd lie there, thinking of all the photos I could take, all the scenes I wanted to capture. This camera quickly became my obsession, and I knew I couldn't hold onto Javed's DSLR forever.

Eventually, the day came when I had to return it, and handing it back felt like giving away a part of myself. But even without the camera in my hands, I couldn't stop thinking about it. I'd go through my day imagining how each scene would look through that lens. The idea of owning a DSLR of my own became all I could think about. Day and night, I'd dream about it—the feel of it in my hands, the thrill of capturing a perfect shot.

Chapter 14: Chasing the Obsession

After my obsession with DSLRs took over, I realized I needed my own, but with no source of income, the only way to get one was to ask my parents. It wasn't something I was used to doing, but I was desperate. So, I gathered all the courage I could muster and approached my father with the request. I remember the way he listened to me patiently, and for a moment, I thought he might understand. But then, the answer came quickly and firmly—a strict "no." He looked at me and said, "We've sent you there to study, not to waste your time with things like cameras."

That rejection hit me hard, but I wasn't ready to give up just yet. I tried again. Day after day, I pleaded with my parents. Every day, I'd find some excuse to bring it up, hoping to convince them that it was more than just a passing fancy. I explained how passionate I was about photography, how important it felt to me to have my own camera. It was like pushing against a wall that wasn't going to budge. My father remained resolute in his response, no matter how much I begged. Every time, the answer was the same—"No, focus on your studies."

It felt like an endless cycle of pleading, and each "no" made me more determined, but also more frustrated. I couldn't explain it to them in a way that made sense to them. To them, a DSLR wasn't a necessity; it was an unnecessary expense, a distraction.

Then, something unexpected happened. After months of me asking, my mother—who was always the softer one—began to show signs of breaking. She had watched me persistently ask, and I think, in her own way, she understood how much it meant to me. I don't know if it was the way I kept coming back to the topic, or maybe it was the desperation she saw in my eyes. Whatever it was, one day she handed me the money. She didn't say anything, but her actions spoke volumes. In that moment, I knew she had finally given in. I felt a wave of relief wash over me, but it was mixed with a deep sense of gratitude. It wasn't just about the camera; it was about the fact that someone had finally listened to me, understood how much this meant to me, and was willing to support it.

With that money, I was ready. I went straight to the store and bought the cheapest DSLR I could find. It wasn't the high-end, feature-packed model I had dreamed of, but it was enough. It was mine. And that feeling of holding my very own DSLR, the one thing I had wanted for so long, was indescribable. There was a sense of accomplishment in that moment—a feeling that I had finally achieved something real. Something that was just for me.

From that moment on, I carried the camera everywhere. It didn't matter where I was going—I took it with me. I started taking pictures of everything: the trees on campus, the bustling streets, the faces of strangers passing by. The world seemed different now, more vibrant, more full of life. With the camera in my hands, I could see things that I hadn't noticed before. Every scene felt like an opportunity to capture something beautiful. The ordinary became extraordinary through the lens, and I realized that the world was full of moments just waiting to be captured.

But it wasn't just about taking random photos. I wanted to learn how to use this new tool the right way. I knew there was more to it than just pointing and shooting, so I turned to YouTube. I spent hours watching tutorials—learning how to adjust settings, how to compose better shots, how to work with lighting, and how to capture the world in a way that told a story. Every video taught me something new, and each lesson felt like a small victory. I was no longer just clicking the shutter; I was learning the art of photography, and every new technique I mastered made me feel more confident.

The camera quickly became my obsession. I would spend hours experimenting with different settings, trying to capture the perfect shot. I would return to the same location multiple times, trying to recreate a shot I had envisioned in my mind. Sometimes, I would even take photos late at night, just because I couldn't put the camera down. I would lie awake, thinking about the next shot, the next angle, the next perfect picture. It wasn't just a hobby anymore—it was a part of me. It felt like I was constantly in pursuit of something bigger, something better. I would imagine the perfect picture in my head, and then set out to capture it. Every time I clicked the shutter, it felt like a small victory—a moment when I had captured something special, something unique.

Chapter 15 :
The Unexpected Shift

While I was immersing myself in the world of photography, something completely unexpected happened—something that would shift my entire focus. It was one of those long, late-night YouTube binges, where I was mindlessly scrolling for new techniques and tips to help improve my photography skills, when I stumbled upon a series of videos by Dr. Najeeb. Now, to give you some context, Dr. Najeeb isn't just another educator; he's a medical teacher renowned for his ability to break down complex topics in a way that actually makes sense. He specializes in medical subjects, and what stood out to me was how different his approach was from anything I had experienced before.

At that point in my life, my relationship with medicine was shallow at best. I was a medical student, yes, but I had long since lost interest in my studies. I had sat through countless lectures, but they felt like a blur—just another hour of my life wasted. I would often show up empty-handed, no books, no notes, no intention to pay attention. If I'm being honest, I would go just to pass the time, or more often than not, to catch up on sleep. The lectures were filled with terms and concepts that went completely over my head, and I couldn't make any sense of them. It wasn't that I didn't want to understand; it was that no matter how hard I tried, I just couldn't connect the dots. I'd sit there, disinterested, wondering how this could possibly be relevant to my future.

But Dr. Najeeb was different. He had this unique ability to take the most complicated medical concepts and break them down into something that wasn't just understandable, but actually fascinating. He didn't teach in the way I had become accustomed to. There were no dry memorization drills or overwhelming lists of facts to cram. Instead, he would explain things in simple, relatable terms. He used analogies and visual aids that made everything click. The way he explained things—it wasn't about just learning for the sake of passing exams; it was about truly understanding how everything fit together, how each piece of knowledge connected to the next. For the first time, I was seeing medicine through a different lens. And suddenly, I was interested.

The change was almost immediate. I began to truly understand biology and medicine in a way I never had before. It felt like I was finally waking up from a long sleep, and I could see things clearly for the first time. I was hooked. I could no longer just sit passively in class; I was hungry for knowledge. And so, I started making notes—something I had never done before. The person who once skipped lectures and ignored textbooks was now sitting down every day, writing pages of notes furiously as I watched Dr.

Najeeb's videos. This wasn't just passive learning; this was active engagement.

It was unbelievable. I had always thought I was someone who didn't care about my medical studies, but here I was, completely invested. My focus shifted dramatically. I found myself revisiting subjects I had previously avoided, trying to understand every detail, no matter how small. The things I had once found boring and difficult, I was now diving into with enthusiasm. It felt surreal to be so involved with something that just months ago seemed impossible to care about.

For the first time in nearly a year and a half, I walked into the library, something I never thought I'd do. The thought of spending hours pouring over textbooks, studying late into the night, was something I had never imagined for myself. But there I was, sitting in the library, surrounded by medical books, feeling determined and motivated. Dr. Najeeb's videos had ignited a spark in me, and I was ready to fan the flames.

Every day, I would watch Dr. Najeeb's videos with renewed enthusiasm. I would pause and rewind, making sure I understood every point he made. It felt like I was uncovering a new world of knowledge, one that was just waiting to be discovered. The more I learned, the more I realized how much I had missed in my past years of study. It was like I had finally unlocked the secret to understanding medical science.

Every day, my confidence grew. I wasn't just preparing to pass the exams—I was certain that I was going to top the upcoming exams. It wasn't just about acing my exams anymore. I started to set my sights on something bigger: cracking the **USMLE**. I knew it was tough—an extremely challenging exam that only the best could pass. But with the way I was understanding medicine now, I was confident that I would make it.

Now, for those who don't know, the USMLE is the gateway for any international medical graduate who wishes to practice medicine in the United States. It's a highly competitive, grueling series of exams that test not just medical knowledge but also your ability to apply that knowledge in real-world scenarios. To say it's hard would be an understatement—it's one of the toughest exams in the world, and only the best can crack it.

Chapter 16: The Reality Check

The day of the exams arrived, and I walked into the exam hall with a level of confidence that could only be described as *unshakable*. I was sure, almost *too sure*, that this was going to be my year. "This year, I'm the one. The topper. Everyone will know my name," I thought. I had prepared. I had watched every single one of Dr. Najeeb's videos. I had made my notes. I had done what I thought was impossible—actually learned something. I was pumped. This was *my* time to shine.

I sat down at my desk, took a deep breath, and opened the exam paper. There it was, the first question. I was ready to conquer it, I thought. But as my eyes scanned the words, my brain did something I hadn't prepared for. It completely blanked out. One second, I was feeling like a genius, the next—*poof*—nothing.

I stared at the question like it was written in an alien language. I could hear the faint hum of the ceiling fan, and then it happened: *complete silence* inside my head. I had no idea what I was looking at. All those hours of Dr. Najeeb's lectures—those enlightening explanations—vanished as if they had been wiped from my brain. The words from those videos, which had felt so clear when I was sitting in my room taking notes, now seemed like they belonged in a completely different universe. *What happened? Where did all that information go?*

I froze, staring blankly at the question. I could hear the clock ticking, each second feeling like an eternity. "Okay, no need to panic," I thought, trying to remain calm. *This is just a momentary lapse.* I tried to think back, to recall everything I had learned, but my mind was empty. The material that had been *so vivid* just hours ago felt completely inaccessible, like trying to reach for a star that was too far out of reach.

I tried to force my brain to work, but the harder I tried, the more I realized that nothing was coming. The more I tried to focus, the more my confidence slipped away. This wasn't how it was supposed to go. *This wasn't the plan.* The "I've-got-this" attitude I had walked in with was now replaced with an overwhelming sense of dread.

An hour passed, and I still hadn't answered a single question. My mind was in full-on panic mode, and my confidence was evaporating faster than my hopes of getting an easy pass. What went wrong? Why couldn't I remember anything? Was this some kind of cosmic joke?

And then, as the minutes ticked away, I remembered something: my old strategy. The strategy that had worked in the past, though not in the way I'd ever hoped. It wasn't perfect, but it worked. Luck. And maybe, just a little bit of "help" here and there.

Somehow, I managed to finish the exam. My mind was numb by the time I handed in my paper. It wasn't a victory. It wasn't a moment of triumph. I didn't feel like I had conquered the exam. Instead, I felt empty. *This wasn't what I had promised myself. This wasn't how I wanted to end this chapter.*

The results came a few weeks later, and to my surprise, I passed. I had somehow scraped through. But when I looked at that passing grade, it didn't feel like a success. It felt hollow. Like I hadn't earned it. I hadn't conquered anything. I had just survived. And I knew, deep down, that this wasn't the path I wanted to follow.

Chapter 17: Rediscovering Passion - From Stagnation to Motion

After the exam disaster, I found myself returning to the place that had always been my comfort zone—photography. It was like slipping back into a familiar rhythm, one that I had put aside when I tried to focus on medicine. Photography had always been my escape, a way to express myself without words. I'd dive into

YouTube tutorials, each one teaching me something new—whether it was playing with lighting, perfecting compositions, or experimenting with editing styles. The thrill of learning a new skill and applying it was refreshing, almost like I was reclaiming a part of myself.

Once again, I was spending hours capturing images, sharing my work on Facebook, and watching the likes and comments roll in. Every positive comment felt like validation. Friends and family would compliment my photos, saying things like, "You really have an eye for this," or, "Your photos capture such unique moments." Their words kept me going. But even with the encouragement, there was a point where I started to feel stuck. I knew I had reached a level of skill, but I wasn't growing past it. No matter how many videos I watched or photos I clicked, the excitement was starting to wear off. There was this feeling—something between frustration and boredom—whenever I held my camera.

I didn't want to admit it, but I had plateaued. I was longing to learn more, to do something different. Photography was no longer giving me that rush it once had. And that's when I stumbled upon video production.

At first, I thought, "How different could it be from photography?" But I soon realized that video production was a completely new world. Photography captures a single moment—a still, silent slice of life. Video, on the other hand, is dynamic; it's like telling a story in real time, where you can play with sound, movement, and pacing. Each frame becomes a part of something larger. Video production was both thrilling and intimidating. I felt like a beginner all over again, but that was exactly what I needed.

The first step was learning the basics of video shooting. How to frame shots differently from photos, adjusting for movement and flow. I had to think about more than just lighting and composition; now I was thinking about pacing, continuity, and how each shot would connect to the next. It was challenging, but I loved every second of it. It was like unlocking a new layer of creativity. The thrill of capturing life as it unfolded, adding sound, tweaking the mood with effects—it was addictive. I started spending hours just exploring Adobe Premiere, trying different effects, learning how to sync background music with the visuals, playing with transitions and color grading.

My room turned into a mini editing studio. My walls were lined with notes about techniques, tutorials, ideas for shots, and lists of music I could use. I was diving deep, and it felt incredible. Instead of simply capturing a single moment, I was now capturing entire scenes, stories, and emotions. The more I learned, the more I realized just how vast the world of video production was. There was so much to explore, from sound design to complex editing techniques, each detail adding depth to the final piece.

I began to love the process—planning shots, experimenting with transitions, adding layers of sound and effects. There was this sense of control and creativity that was unmatched. I would shoot random clips, edit them into mini videos, add some music, and then post them online. The response was amazing. People were starting to notice. They'd comment on how my videos made them feel something different, how my storytelling had grown. And every time someone left a positive comment, it felt like fuel to keep pushing further.

Slowly but surely, my passion had shifted from photography to video production. It wasn't about capturing single moments anymore; it was about creating experiences, building stories. I could express so much more through videos than I ever could with just photos. What started as a curiosity quickly turned into an obsession. I was drawn into this new world, one where I felt like I was truly growing again, learning something new every day.

Chapter 18: Chasing Viral Dreams

While I was getting deeper into the world of video production, something interesting was happening on a much bigger scale. YouTube was exploding in India, and everyone was talking about it. Creators were suddenly becoming celebrities, especially the ones who made funny, relatable content. These "Viners" were hilarious, making everyone laugh with everyday humor, simple scenarios, and clever dialogue. People were hooked on short comedy sketches, and some of these "YouTubers" were gaining millions of views practically overnight. It felt like anyone with a camera and a sense of humor could become famous. And I thought, *Why not me?*

So, I decided to give it a shot. If others could do it, why couldn't I? I started writing some comedy scripts, planning out scenes, and thinking about characters. I roped in a few of my batchmates, who were surprisingly enthusiastic. We would gather in our dorm or a nearby spot to shoot, and let me tell you, it was a blast. We'd spend hours laughing over the characters I created, the lines they had to say, and the silly expressions they had to make. Every line would have us breaking into fits of laughter, and I thought, If we're laughing this much, people are going to love it too.

We spent hours filming, often having to reshoot scenes because we'd start laughing in the middle of a take. I can't tell you how much fun those shoots were—it didn't feel like work at all. It felt like hanging out with friends, making each other laugh, and capturing the best moments on camera.

After hours of laughter, I'd finally have enough footage to edit. I'd sit down, add some effects, sync up the dialogues, and polish it as best I could. I felt like I had created something great, something funny that people would love. I could already imagine the views rolling in, people sharing it everywhere, maybe even getting messages from random fans. The anticipation was almost as thrilling as making the video itself.

Then came the big moment. I uploaded the video to YouTube, hit publish, and waited. I kept refreshing the page, watching the views with excitement. I was ready to see the numbers shoot up, waiting for the flood of views and comments that would validate all our hard work. But as the hours went by, I realized the view count wasn't exactly soaring. Instead of thousands of views, I was getting a few hundred—mostly from friends, family, and people who knew me. In the end, that first video got around 500-600 view. I told myself it was a learning experience. *Maybe the video wasn't good enough*, I thought. *No worries, I'll do better next time.*

Determined, I wrote another script, one I thought was even funnier, and again, gathered my friends for another round of laughs and filming. This time, we put even more effort into it, laughing until our stomachs hurt and having an absolute blast. Once again, I spent hours editing, refining every little detail, polishing the video to make sure it was even better than the last. The jokes were tighter, and I felt like this video had all the ingredients to go viral. I uploaded it, convinced this was the one that would change everything. I pictured thousands of views, then hundreds of thousands, maybe even a million.

This time, the video managed to get around 1100 views. Better than the last one, but still far from my viral dreams. I kept thinking, *Maybe it just takes time.* But deep down, I was beginning to wonder if it was going to happen at all.

Still, I wasn't one to give up easily. I decided to try again, this time putting in even more effort. I spent days writing a script, trying to make it perfect, adding little details I thought would make it funnier, and working on each character until I was sure they were hilarious. We filmed the video, had as much fun as ever, and I once again dove into the editing process with a sense of purpose. I thought to myself, *This is the one. This is the video that's going to go viral.*

I uploaded it, took a deep breath, and waited. This time, the video got around 400 views.

That was the moment I realized that going viral wasn't as simple as I had thought. It wasn't enough to just make a funny video and throw it online. There were thousands of people doing the exact same thing, all competing for the same audience. Maybe my content wasn't reaching people because I didn't understand the platform, or maybe because it didn't have that "something extra." But one thing was clear: going viral wasn't just about uploading a video and waiting for the magic to happen.

I didn't exactly quit making funny videos after that, but I stopped expecting that overnight success. Instead, I shifted my focus back to what I had genuinely come to love: the art and process of creating videos themselves.

Chapter 19: The Final Year Crisis

While I was busy making videos, experimenting with edits, and immersing myself in every aspect of production, fourth year crept up on me like a shadow. I hadn't realized how quickly the years had passed until I suddenly found myself on the edge of graduation. The moment felt like a wake-up call, and the carefree days of filming and editing seemed like a bubble about to burst.

The real world loomed large, demanding answers. As a kid, I had always thought adults knew exactly what they were doing, but here I was—just months from becoming a doctor—without a clue about what my future held. Sure, I'd trained in medicine, but my heart wasn't in it. I was good at creating videos, but a haunting question kept echoing in my mind: Could I ever make a living doing this?

That's when the anxiety started tightening its grip. At first, it was subtle—just a few nagging questions at the back of my mind. But soon, those questions turned into full-blown doubts that consumed my days and kept me up at night. What would I do after I graduated? How would I earn a living?

Depression settled in like an unwelcome guest. By day, I pretended everything was fine. I attended classes, hung out with friends, and even kept making videos, but inside, I was struggling. Around me, friends were discussing their career plans, deciding which specialty to pursue in post-graduation, while I felt completely lost. It seemed like everyone else had life figured out, and I was the only one stumbling in the dark.

Each night, I would lay in bed, staring at the ceiling, wondering what would happen to me after graduation. Could I truly support myself doing what I loved? It felt like standing on the edge of a cliff, staring down into an uncertain future without a clue how to move forward.

Every time I tried to plan my future, I felt trapped, caught between two worlds. On one side was the medical field—stable, secure, but passionless for me. On the other was the world of video production, which filled me with energy but didn't promise a steady paycheck. I started questioning every choice I'd made. Nights were the worst—lying in bed, alone with my fears. That's when the voices in my head grew louder, replaying every misstep, every regret.

The thought of failing became this dark cloud that followed me everywhere. I could imagine the looks on people's faces if I stumbled, the whispers behind my back, the disappointed nods. I pictured people saying, "He should have just stuck to medicine. What's he doing with these videos?" My future felt like a monster, closing in on me no matter how fast I tried to outrun it.

I would sit with my camera and editing software, trying to find comfort in the one thing I truly loved. But even that began to lose its spark. The fear of an uncertain future seeped into everything, tainting even my passion. I tried to drown my worries in editing, cutting, and adding music, but it was like trying to hold back a flood with a cup. The doubt was relentless, breaking through every attempt I made to ignore it.

More than anything, I just wanted to believe in a future where I could do what I loved without struggling to survive. I didn't need fame or fortune—just enough to live a simple life, enough to make a modest living doing what I enjoyed. But every time I thought about the future, it seemed like a mirage, slipping further out of reach. I was spiraling, caught in a loop of self-doubt and fear, with no answers in sight. And the more I searched for them, the further they seemed to slip away.

As graduation drew closer, the fear only grew. I was stuck in a cycle of worries, chasing answers that felt impossible to find.

Chapter 20: A Message in the Dark

So there I was, in my final year, drowning in the fog of confusion. Depression was already weighing me down, and on top of that, I had no idea what I wanted to do with my life. Medicine just wasn't for me, but everyone around me had such high expectations. I felt stuck, unable to tell anyone that I wanted something different. I knew I needed a change, but where would I even begin?

One night, as I was scrolling through Facebook, something unusual caught my eye. A travel agency had posted an ad, and they were looking for someone to document their trips. My heart skipped a beat. They'd pay me to travel and make videos? This was exactly what I'd been dreaming about—a chance to explore, make films, and maybe find a purpose outside of medicine. Without a second thought, I applied for that position, feeling a spark of excitement I hadn't felt in a long time.

Days passed, then weeks, with no response. That silence was disheartening, but instead of letting it get me down, it gave me an idea. What if I reached out to other agencies to see if they had similar work? It was a long shot, but I had nothing to lose. With renewed determination, I searched Facebook for travel agencies, sending messages one by one. Each message was carefully written, highlighting my passion for videography and eagerness to work.

I repeated this routine every day for nearly three months. Some days, I spent hours straight on Facebook, eyes glued to the screen as I crafted each message. My hands would ache from typing, but I kept going. Sometimes I wondered if it was worth the effort, but deep down, I knew that I had to try everything to make this happen.

After weeks of waiting and hundreds of messages, I was starting to lose hope. Then, out of nowhere, a reply popped up. One travel agency had finally responded, and they had a job for me. They told me they had a group tour going to Manali and needed a videographer. It was exactly what I'd been waiting for.

Then they mentioned the budget: ☐15,000.

The agency seemed hesitant, almost as if they were expecting me to say, "☐15,000? That's too low. Can we raise the budget a bit?" But they didn't know how desperate I was for an opportunity, how long I'd waited for this moment. In my mind, ☐15,000 was more than enough. It was my first job, and I immediately said yes, leaving them slightly surprised—and maybe even a bit relieved.

Soon I was packing my bags to travel all the way from Patna to Delhi to join their trip.

This was my first real gig in videography, and I was beyond excited. The experience didn't disappoint. Manali was beautiful, and filming the tour felt like a dream come true. I couldn't believe that I was actually getting paid for something that didn't feel like work. It was just me, my camera, and a stunning landscape in front of me.

During that trip, I met rahul, another travel agency owner. He hinted at future work opportunities. But that's a story for later.

After the trip, I delivered the video to the agency, feeling proud of what I had created. To my relief, they loved it. Watching their reaction to my work was one of the best feelings I'd ever experienced, and I realized that maybe this path was something I could actually pursue.

That first project didn't just give me a paycheck; it gave me confidence. It was proof that there could be a future for me beyond medicine—a path I could carve myself, on my own terms.

Chapter 21: The Countdown to Freedom

While I was still figuring out what to do with my life, the final year exams approached faster than I expected. My usual approach had been to rely on a mix of luck, quick glances at neighboring answers, and some strategic positioning. But this time, things took a serious turn. Our college had implemented strict measures: the seating arrangement were strict, invigilators were vigilant, making it impossible to get any help or glance over at anyone's paper. I realized, too late, that this time I was on my own.

On the day of the first exam, I remember walking into the hall and feeling an overwhelming sense of dread. I took my seat and looked around, realizing that for the first time, I'd be on my own. A few hours later, I walked out, already fearing the worst. The rest of the exams went just as badly—I simply didn't know the material. I'd managed to scrape by in past years, but now it seemed the years of shortcuts had caught up with me.

When the results were finally announced, my worst fear became reality: I had failed in four out of five subjects. My friends and batchmates were moving forward with internships and real-world experiences, leaving me behind. While they celebrated and posted updates about their next steps, I was left facing what felt like a ticking time bomb.

Supplementary exams were scheduled for three months later, and if I didn't pass, I'd be stuck in a loop, doomed to repeat the entire year. Just the thought was suffocating. A year back meant one more year in a course I desperately wanted to leave, one more year watching everyone else move ahead while I stayed stuck.

There was one more twist to the nightmare: the setup for supplementary exams was even stricter. The exams were held in near-empty rooms, with only a handful of students scattered throughout. No distractions, no crowd, and certainly no help from a classmate. In fact, the other students in the room were in the same boat as I was—equally lost and probably just as desperate. I couldn't rely on anyone but myself. It was clear I had to face this one head-on, or I'd be staring at another year of frustration, confinement, and stalled dreams.

For the first time in two years, I pulled out my textbooks and really started studying. There was no other option. I knew nothing, and there was no time for shortcuts. I spent those months cramming material, struggling to retain information I'd neglected for years, and pushing myself harder than I ever had before. I wanted to be done, to be free of this place, and the only way out was through those exams.

Finally, the supplementary exams arrived. As I walked into the exam hall, I felt the weight of everything on my shoulders. This was my last shot. I could almost feel the stakes—one misstep, one failed answer, and I'd be stuck here for another year. When the papers were handed out, I took a deep breath and dove in, determined to give it everything I had.

Weeks passed as I waited for the results, the anxiety building each day. When the results day finally arrived, my hands were shaking as I opened the portal. My mind raced through all the "what-ifs"— what if I didn't pass, what if all those hours weren't enough, what if this place would keep me trapped for another year?

But there it was, clear as day: I had passed. And for the first time, I had done it entirely on my own—no shortcuts, no borrowed answers, just my effort. It was a relief like no other, and in that moment, I knew I could push through anything if I put in the work.

Chapter 22: The Internship Dilemma

After finally clearing my final exams, I entered my internship year, a time I thought might bring relief from the chaos and pressures of med school. No more exams, just hands-on training. But the reality hit me differently. Each day, I was expected to spend 8 to 10 hours rotating between the OPD and the operation theaters. And every time I walked through those hospital corridors, I felt like an imposter. I was supposed to be learning, but I wasn't picking things up, and instead of curiosity, I felt a strange detachment. I became almost allergic to the place.

The worst part? Professors constantly firing questions my way. Every time they asked something, it felt like a spotlight on all the things I didn't know. I'd end up mumbling something or blankly staring, hoping the questions would move to someone else. The whole atmosphere just made me feel more and more alienated from the medical field. I was trapped in a place where I couldn't see my future, yet I was expected to grind through it, day after day.

Then one day, as I was mentally planning my next excuse to skip a day, I got a message from rahul, the guy I'd met on my first videography gig to Manali. He said he had a new project for me—a corporate trip heading to Haridwar—and he wanted me to cover it. That message was like a breath of fresh air, a small escape from the hospital and the questions I couldn't answer. Without hesitation, I told him I'd do it.

Getting four days off was a hassle, but I managed it and made my way to Haridwar. The project went great, and I enjoyed every moment, soaking in the break from the hospital. This felt like where I was meant to be—capturing moments, creating something real. After delivering the final video to rahul, I asked about my payment, feeling that this was my first step toward building a career that was actually meaningful to me.

But rahul's response caught me off guard. "Some of my payments are stuck right now, but I'll clear yours with the next project," he said. I was disappointed, but I thought maybe he was just going through a rough patch. A month passed, and rahul reached out again with another project—this time a corporate trip to Kasol. I wanted to believe that I'd be paid for both projects this time, so I agreed to cover the trip. Again, I completed the work and delivered the video, expecting that this time, everything would go smoothly.

But when I asked for my payment, he came up with a different excuse: "Someone committed fraud with my company recently.

Don't worry, though—I'll pay you after the next project." That sinking feeling started to build up.

Another month later, he reached out with yet another project. By now, I was wary. I was frustrated and, honestly, starting to feel a bit foolish for believing him. But rahul assured me that he'd settle all pending payments right after this project. He sounded confident, and I wanted so badly to believe him. So, reluctantly, I took on the project, thinking this would finally be the one where he'd come through.

I poured my effort into it, completed the video, and handed it over. Then I waited. And when I finally asked about the payment, his reply was another excuse—a vague story that felt like he hadn't even put effort into making it sound believable. That was the breaking point. I realized rahul had no intention of paying me and that I'd been foolish in trusting him time and again.

The frustration of those unpaid projects weighed on me heavily. It wasn't just about the money. It was the realization that in my eagerness to escape the hospital and pursue something I loved, I'd allowed myself to be taken advantage of. rahul had been a lesson—a harsh one—on valuing my work and standing my ground. After that, I stopped taking his calls and rejected any further projects he offered.

Back in the hospital, as I returned to my routine of dodging questions and counting down the hours, I felt the sting of reality. The money I'd counted on to start my videography journey was lost, and my chance to escape the hospital routine felt further away than ever. But that experience also planted something important in me: a resolve to do things differently, to work smarter, and to never undervalue my efforts again.

Chapter 23: Choosing the Path Less Taken

As my internship was coming to an end, I found myself standing at a crossroads, facing a decision that felt impossible to make. I had spent years in the medical field, studying and working hard, but deep down, I knew it wasn't where I belonged. My parents, like many others, had pinned their hopes on me pursuing a career in medicine. It was a well-worn, reliable path that promised stability, and they believed it was the right way forward. They kept saying, "Beta, ek baar PG kar lo, uske baad jo karna hai, kar lena (complete your post-graduation first, after that, you can do whatever you want)"—a line I'd heard a thousand times. In their view, completing post-graduate medical studies would offer a safety net, something I could fall back on no matter what happened next.

But I could feel my soul slowly draining every day I spent in the medical field. It wasn't just about the work itself—it was the pressure, the routine, and the lack of passion. I wasn't excited to wake up in the morning; I was counting down the days. The thought of continuing down this path, of being stuck in a career I had no love for, was terrifying. I knew that if I didn't make a change, I'd only end up unhappy, possibly even mentally broken. It was like a part of me was screaming to be freed from the medical world, to find something that made me feel alive.

Even though my parents' advice was rooted in love and concern, I couldn't ignore the deep sense of dissatisfaction I felt. Video production, something I had always been passionate about, was calling me. It was the only thing I knew that made me feel truly alive. Whenever I thought about video, about creating stories and capturing moments, it gave me a sense of purpose that medicine never could. I realized then that I had to give it a real shot, no matter how uncertain the future looked.

When I finally sat down to talk to my parents about this decision, I knew it wasn't going to be easy. Their reaction was exactly what I had expected. "Whatever you want to do, you'll have to do it on your own," they said. "We won't support you in this." The words stung, but I also understood where they were coming from. They had spent years supporting me in my medical studies, and now I was about to throw it all away for something that didn't guarantee a stable future.

While most of my friends and peers were either securing stable jobs or preparing for further studies, I was about to step into an unknown world. A world where I didn't have connections, experience, or any of the usual advantages. It was a world that seemed to offer more risks than rewards. But I had something that others didn't: an unshakeable passion for video production and a deep belief that this was my true calling.

I knew it wasn't going to be easy. But I also knew that if I didn't take this chance, I would always regret it. I didn't have a backup plan, and I didn't want one. I was determined to make it on my own terms, even if that meant going through hard times. It wasn't just about making a living; it was about living in a way that felt true to myself. I was ready to step out of my comfort zone and face whatever challenges came my way.

Chapter 24: Finding My Path

As I made the decision to step into the world of video production, a thousand questions ran through my mind. The most pressing one was how I would earn a living. After doing some research and thinking about it deeply, I realized there were typically three main ways to make money in this industry.

First, there was the **wedding segment**. Wedding videography is an extremely popular business, and many people make good money from it. However, the downside is that wedding clients are often unprofessional, unorganized, and the work can sometimes feel monotonous. The pressure to satisfy demanding clients, especially when they have unrealistic expectations, didn't seem like the right fit for me. While the money might have been good, it didn't align with my aspirations or values.

Second, there was the **content industry** – creating films, documentaries, and TV shows. This is the most glamorous part of video production for many, but it's also the most competitive. There are thousands of talented filmmakers out there, each trying to make a name in an already overcrowded space. The industry is filled with people who have years of experience, connections, and resources that I didn't have. Even though the thought of working in film excited me, I didn't have the confidence to dive in headfirst, not knowing where to start or how to stand out in such a saturated field.

Then there was the **commercial segment**, which seemed to have the most potential for me. This segment included corporate videos, advertisements, promotional videos, and product shoots. The demand was huge, especially with businesses looking for ways to connect with their audience through professional videos. However, the competition was much lower compared to the wedding or content industry.

So I decided to focus on this commercial segment. It felt like the most logical choice, especially considering the growing demand from businesses. I knew that if I could deliver great work to just a few clients, word would spread, and more opportunities would follow.

The decision wasn't easy. I had no formal experience or connections in the commercial video industry. I didn't know where to start or how to find clients. But I knew I had to take the leap. I had to start somewhere, and the commercial world seemed like a fertile ground to begin my journey.

Chapter 25: A Risky Partnership

Without the luxury of parental support, I now needed a solid plan. While opportunities for video production were limited locally, I was constantly searching for ways to break into the industry. That's when it hit me: maybe I could find someone in Delhi NCR who could handle the business side of things. Delhi was a hub for media opportunities, and if I could partner with someone experienced in bringing in clients, I might actually have a shot at making this dream a reality.

I posted in a few Facebook groups, explaining that I was looking for a business partner who could help me bring in projects. Before long, a guy named vishal responded. He was working as a business developer for a web development company, managing client relationships and bringing in new business. He seemed confident that he could do the same for me and was eager to take on the role. Soon enough, he started sending a few small projects my way, which made me feel like partnering with vishal might just be the breakthrough I was hoping for.

As soon as my internship ended, I didn't waste any time. With only ☐16,000 in my pocket, I packed my bags and moved to Noida to give this partnership a real shot. Thankfully, my cousin who already lived there agreed to share his flat with me, so that took some financial pressure off my shoulders. The flat rent was ☐16,000 a month, so my share came to ☐8,000. I knew I had maybe a month or two to survive if I spent carefully, but I was too focused on making this work to worry about the risk.

Those first few days in Delhi were overwhelming. Vishal was full of energy, talking about how we should register a company to make everything official. Although I felt uneasy about spending my limited funds on registration fees, he convinced me it was the right step. "This is how real businesses start," he said. Trusting him, I went along with it, thinking we were building something solid together.

However, after getting the company registered, things changed almost immediately. vishal, who had seemed so driven and full of ideas, suddenly went quiet. He stopped bringing in projects, barely responded to my messages, and started focusing more on his previous job. I tried to stay optimistic, assuming he'd eventually come around, but as the days turned into weeks, it was clear that nothing was changing.

With no help from vishal, I found myself working non-stop, pitching to anyone willing to listen. I spent hours each day glued to my phone and laptop, hustling for any project I could land. Some small projects finally started coming in, and for a moment, I thought I could breathe easier. But that was when vishal started demanding half of every payment that came in. Despite not contributing anything, he felt entitled to 50% because clients were paying us through our company account, which he had conveniently registered under both our names.

I tried to convince myself that maybe he'd start pulling his weight, that things would balance out eventually. But the frustration grew with each passing day. I was burning through my savings, working tirelessly, while vishal seemed perfectly content taking his half without lifting a finger.

After two or three projects, I reached my breaking point. I couldn't ignore the reality any longer—this partnership wasn't just unbalanced; it was taking a toll on me emotionally and financially. One evening, I confronted vishal, explaining how unfair this arrangement had become. The conversation quickly turned heated, as he refused to acknowledge any fault. It was clear he had no intention of putting in the work.

That's when I realized he was only in it for the easy money, nothing more. It was a hard pill to swallow, but I knew I had to act. I told him I was done. I'd rather face the unknown alone than continue a partnership that felt more like a burden than a stepping stone.

Walking away from that partnership wasn't easy, but once I made the decision, it felt like a huge weight had been lifted off my shoulders. For the first time, I felt free to pursue this journey on my own terms. It was a tough lesson, but one that gave me a renewed sense of determination. From that point on, I knew if I was going to make it, it would be through my own strength, my own hustle. The path ahead was unknown, but I felt ready to face it head-on, carrying forward the hard-earned wisdom that some partnerships are best left behind.

Chapter 26: The Struggles Days

The first year of running my own business was nothing short of a survival game. I'd wake up at 8 in the morning and start cold-calling companies and potential clients by 9 AM. I didn't have any network, no connections—just my phone and a lot of hope. I'd keep calling until 9 PM every single day, trying to convince people to give me a chance. My entire day revolved around getting someone, anyone, to say yes. But instead, I heard "No" hundreds of times.

It was exhausting. By the end of each day, my head would be throbbing, and my phone, which was an old Android model, would often hang from overuse. But I didn't stop. I couldn't. Cold-calling was the only way I knew to reach people. Every call that was cut short, every polite rejection, every rude dismissal—it all added up, making me feel like I was fighting an uphill battle alone. I didn't know any other way, though, so I pushed through.

Financially, things were rough. There were days when I simply didn't have money to buy food, so I'd go to sleep on an empty stomach. The hunger was a constant reminder of how things were going for me. It was hard not to feel defeated, especially when I was putting in all this effort without much to show for it. Still, I had no choice but to keep going.

One incident sticks out from that year. One of my cousins invited me to her birthday. I had just ☐500 on me, and that was everything I had in the world at that moment. I could have just shown up without a gift, but I didn't want to look cheap in front of my family. So, I bought a small gift worth ☐420 and was left with only ☐80. That ☐80 was supposed to last me for the next 10-12 days, and somehow, I made it work. I had to carefully plan every rupee—eating less and only when absolutely necessary. I wouldn't even let myself think about spending anything extra.

Each month, as the rent due date came closer, the stress would build up. I'd look at my bank balance and wonder how I was going to make it. My landlord wasn't someone who'd let things slide, and I couldn't risk getting thrown out. I'd feel that anxiety pile up as the days passed. But somehow, by what felt like a miracle, some payment or small project would come through just in time. It was never more than just enough to cover the rent and some basic needs, but that was enough for me to survive another month.

Looking back, it felt like there was a higher power watching over me during those days, making sure I got just enough to keep going. I don't know if it was luck, hard work, or just fate, but each time, I managed to scrape through by the barest of margins. These little breaks kept my hope alive. They weren't big wins, but they were enough to make me feel like I was still in the game.

In many ways, that first year laid the foundation for everything that came after. Every rejection, every sleepless night, and every bit of hunger was part of a hard lesson in survival, perseverance, and self-belief. It wasn't easy, but those experiences built a strength in me that nothing else could.

Chapter 27: The Early Clients

While I was busy cold-calling marketing agencies to see if they had any work they could pass on to me. Finally, one agency responded, saying they had a client—a well-known jeweler in Chandni Chowk—who needed good photos of his jewelry designs. The agency guy said he would directly connect me to the jeweler and not be involved in any kind of deal. I didn't think much about why the agency wanted to stay out of it, but later, I would understand why.

I went to Chandni Chowk to meet this jeweler in his crowded shop, which was filled with cases of gold and diamond jewelry. He explained that he has around 60 pieces he needed photographed, with each piece captured from 3-4 different angles. Now, photography wasn't my area of expertise, but I couldn't afford to say no to any work at that point. So, I offered to do the job at ₹200 per piece, meaning the entire project would cost ₹12,000. He agreed to this price, and we planned the shoot for the next week.

When I asked for an advance, he hesitated, saying he would pay once the shoot was done. Though I felt unsure, I thought maybe this was just the way some businesses operate, so I went along with it. However, I quickly realized I had a problem—product photography usually requires a lightbox, and the cheapest one I could find was around ₹8,000. I didn't have any other options because, without it, the shoot wouldn't look professional. So, I decided to buy it, figuring that once I got paid, I'd still be left with about ₹4,000, which could help me manage for a few more days in the city.

On the day of the shoot, I took the lightbox and all my gear to his shop. After setting everything up, I got to work, taking 7-8 hours to carefully photograph each piece from multiple angles. The jeweler was watching the entire time, and he seemed happy, even praising my work. But when I asked for an advance before leaving, he tried to brush it off again, saying he'd prefer to pay everything after he saw the final images. I had to stand firm, telling him I couldn't leave without at least half the payment. After some back-and-forth, he finally gave me ₹6,000 in advance.

Feeling relieved, I went back to my flat and spent the next several days editing the photos, putting in hours to make sure they looked sharp and clear. When I sent him the final images, I thought everything was fine. But as soon as he saw the photos, his attitude changed. Suddenly, he started criticizing the photos, calling them "unprofessional" and "blurry." I was confused and asked him to explain what he didn't like about the pictures, but he just kept repeating the same complaints without being specific.

When I asked him to clear the rest of my payment, he flat-out refused, saying he wasn't going to pay me anything more. That's when I realized he had no intention of paying me from the start. If I hadn't insisted on the advance, I would have lost not just my time but also ☐8,000 from buying the lightbox. Even though I was out ☐2,000, at least I hadn't taken a bigger hit. And the funny part? A month later, I saw my photos in his ads. The same photos he claimed were "blurry" were now all over his marketing!

It finally made sense why the agency guy didn't want to be in the middle of this deal. He likely knew the jeweler's reputation for not paying up and didn't want to get involved. It was a hard lesson learned, but it taught me a lot about dealing with clients and standing my ground.

Looking back, this was one of the first times I realized how important it is to be careful and protect myself in business. Trust is important, but so is making sure I don't get taken advantage of, especially as a newcomer just finding my way in this big city.

Chapter 28: The Breaking Point

The first year of running my video production company was nothing like I had imagined. Most of the people I use to call were either uninterested or would just listen politely before cutting the call. It was disheartening, but I knew I had to keep going. Some of the marketing agencies I contacted would actually invite me for meetings, and I would rush there with hope and energy, believing this could be my big break. I would put on my best professional face, traveled across the city, and present my ideas with enthusiasm. But after each meeting, I was met with the same disappointing response: "We'll get back to you." And nothing ever came of it. No project. No follow-up. The disappointment was relentless. Every meeting that ended with no project felt like another nail in the coffin of my hopes.

Even when I did manage to land a client, the real challenge started afterward. Most of them would take the video, look satisfied with the work, and then simply refuse to pay. They'd come up with every excuse in the book, leaving me chasing payments I'd already earned. It wasn't just a few clients—it was almost all of them. I had never imagined that the world I was trying to break into would be this tough. As much as I was giving my all to every project, it felt like the universe was pushing me back. I would work tirelessly to produce quality content, only to see the effort go unpaid.

It was hard not to compare myself to others. While I was hustling day in and day out, I watched my friends effortlessly buy new gadgets, drive fancy cars, and take trips without a care in the world. They were living lives that seemed to be moving forward, while I was stuck in a never-ending cycle of rejection and uncertainty. They talked about the new clothes they bought, the vacations they were planning, and how they were building their futures. Meanwhile, I was still cold calling, attending meetings, and trying to figure out how to make my business work.

There were days when the contrast between their success and my struggle was too much to bear. The weight of it all was heavy, and I began to doubt myself more and more. I felt like I was giving it my all, but with nothing to show for it. My pocket was always empty, and I couldn't even afford the basic things that I needed. I watched as people around me achieved what seemed like effortless success, while I was stuck in a pit of uncertainty, feeling like I was never going to make it out.

My relatives would ask, "How's your production house going?" Every time they asked, I would force a smile and say, "It's going great." I didn't want them to know how broken I felt inside. I didn't want to admit that I was struggling, that I was scared, and that I didn't know how much longer I could keep going. I couldn't bear the thought of them knowing how much I was hurting, so I pretended. I told them everything was fine, even though deep down, I was far from fine. I didn't know how much longer I could keep up the act. The pressure was mounting, and I was running out of strength to hide the truth.

There were many nights when I lay awake, wondering if leaving the medical field had been a mistake. Was this the right path? But every time those doubts crept in, I would remember how unbearable the thought of returning to medicine was. The idea of going back to a life that drained me emotionally and mentally was far worse than facing the uncertainty of this new career. But with every unpaid project, the fear of failure grew stronger. I kept questioning if I was fooling myself by sticking with video production. The fear was always there, a constant companion that whispered to me, questioning whether I had made the right choice.

Then, one day, I hit my breaking point. It was 11 in the morning when my cousin left for work, and I found myself sitting alone. That day, something inside me snapped. I felt like I couldn't hold it in any longer. I broke down. I just started crying. It wasn't just a few tears. It was the kind of crying where you don't know when it's going to stop, where you can't catch your breath, where everything feels like it's too much. I was crying not just because of the endless struggle but because I honestly didn't know where my life was heading. It felt like I had invested everything—emotionally, financially—into something that was taking me nowhere. I was scared and lost, feeling like I had nothing left. It wasn't just a moment of weakness; it felt like a deep, raw breakdown. I cried for hours, trying to process all the frustrations and disappointments that had been building up.

By the time my cousin came back around 6 pm, I had cried for almost seven hours straight. But I stopped because I didn't want him to know how broken I was. In his eyes, I had managed to maintain the image of someone who was doing well, someone who had everything under control. I didn't want to shatter that illusion, especially when I knew that, deep down, I had no answers or solutions. The last thing I wanted was for him to see me as someone who had failed, someone who couldn't even make ends meet. So, I wiped my tears, tried to pull myself together, and greeted him with a smile as if everything was fine.

All I knew was that I was at a crossroads, unsure whether to keep going or walk away from everything. It was one of the hardest days of my life—one where I questioned my choices, my future, and the path I had chosen.

Chapter 29: The Unexpected Shift

While I was struggling to keep things afloat, something unexpected and honestly, pretty shocking, happened—my cousin got transferred to Pune. Until then, we'd been sharing the ☐16,000 rent, a sum that was already pushing my limits. His sudden departure put me in a position I hadn't anticipated. Now, I had to manage the entire rent on my own. It didn't take long for the anxiety to creep in—I had no idea how I'd manage it on my own.

My immediate thought was to find a new flatmate—someone who could share the rent and lighten the load. Without wasting any time, I listed the vacancy, hoping I could find someone quickly. Days turned into weeks, and every day, I'd show the flat to potential flatmates. They'd come, take a look around, and then say they had a few more places to check out. Each time, I'd wait to hear back, but they never did. As the days went by, my nerves started to build up. Without a flatmate, staying there didn't seem sustainable, and I couldn't afford to keep waiting for someone who might never show up.

By the end of those two weeks, reality started to sink in. I couldn't keep waiting around for a flatmate who might never show up. My options were running thin, and the pressure of handling the full rent was growing heavier by the day. I'd started to feel an overwhelming sense of uncertainty about how I was going to make it work. It wasn't just about the rent anymore—it was a question of whether or not I'd even be able to keep living in the city I'd chosen for my dreams.

With no luck finding a flatmate, I decided to look for cheaper flats. I set a maximum rent of ☐8,000, something that would be manageable even without a flatmate. I started visiting flats in that range, hoping I'd find something decent. But each flat was worse than the last. Dimly lit rooms, cramped spaces, questionable plumbing—it felt like I was being asked to give up my dignity and peace just to make ends meet. I realized that moving into one of those spaces would have come with a high cost to my mental well-being.

After several disappointing viewings, I returned to my flat feeling defeated. None of the options in my budget felt remotely like a place I'd be happy to call home. Staying where I was meant living on the edge financially, but moving felt like surrendering a part of myself. I weighed the pros and cons of each decision over and over again. The thought of paying the full ☐16,000 rent alone terrified me, but the alternative didn't seem much better. It felt like a no-win situation.

Finally, I decided to stay in the flat and figure out how to make it work. I knew it would require some sacrifices—I'd have to cut down on other expenses and live as frugally as possible.

The decision to stay didn't make everything magically easier. There were nights I'd lie awake, crunching numbers in my head, wondering how long I could keep this up. The financial strain was constant, and there were moments when I wondered if I'd made the right choice. But each day, I found a little more determination to make it through. My journey in Delhi had always been about pushing boundaries, and this was just another hurdle.

Chapter 30: Taking Matters into My Own Hands

As the pressure of managing my business grew, I found myself struggling more with each passing day. Then one day, my friend Jai came over to visit. Jai worked for a digital marketing company in Noida, and we ended up talking for hours. Eventually, I opened up about the challenges I was facing. I shared how each meeting felt like a shot in the dark, how many clients wouldn't pay, and how I was barely making ends meet. I confessed the harsh reality of my so-called "production house" and even admitted that I was starting to lose faith in my decision to leave medicine.

Jai listened carefully and suggested, "You should consider digital marketing. It could help you reach more clients." I hesitated immediately. To me, digital marketing felt like pouring funds into something with no guaranteed return. In fact, I had tried running some ads on Facebook before, boosting a few posts that got some likes but led to no actual work or client inquiries. It felt pointless, as though I was spending money for a couple of likes and nothing more. If my budget was stretched thin just keeping the business running, how could I justify throwing money at something that might not even bring in clients? Marketing felt like a gamble, and I told him as much. But he explained that, with the right approach, it could bring visibility to my work in a way cold calling never could. He shared examples of small businesses that had turned around simply by having a solid online presence. It struck me that maybe I'd been looking at it all wrong.

Since Jai was already in the digital marketing world, he had a fair idea of what might help a small business like mine gain visibility. He suggested I start by creating a website to establish an online presence. I didn't have much money to spare, especially for something that felt like a "luxury." But Jai was persistent, and the way he explained it made sense. He even offered to connect me with two of his friends who could help me out.

First, he introduced me to Manas, a web developer who would supposedly build my website, and then to Chandan, who could handle the marketing campaigns. Jai's confidence in his friends gave me a bit of hope, and since he was a close friend, I felt like I couldn't say no. So, with whatever little savings I had left, I decided to take the leap. I asked Manas to start working on the website.

Manas told me he'd need about 15 days to deliver a professional, fully-functional website. That seemed reasonable, so I agreed and started waiting. But those 15 days turned into 20, and still, there was no sign of the website. When I reached out, Manas explained that the site he was building was "quite complex" and would need more time. Not wanting to seem impatient, I agreed to wait a bit longer, though frustration was already creeping in.

Weeks went by, and still no website. The next time I asked, he told me he was caught up with his sister's wedding, so things were delayed. It was frustrating—I was spending money on something that didn't even exist yet, and I was starting to feel taken advantage of. It became clear that if I kept waiting, this website might never be ready. So, I decided to take things into my own hands.

I figured that if other people could build websites, maybe I could too. I dove into YouTube tutorials, learning the basics of web design and development, determined to make this work on my own. Manas did give me some guidance here and there, but the bulk of the work—about 80%—was done by me, struggling through one video at a time. After nearly three months, I finally got that website up and running. It was simple, but it felt like a huge achievement—something I had built from scratch.

Once the website was complete, I cleared Manas's payment, even though I had done most of the work myself. At least now I had a digital presence, something to show potential clients.

Chapter 31:
The Digital Marketing Gamble

With the website up and running, the next task was to get the marketing campaigns rolling. Chandan, who was handling the digital marketing side of things, took about a week to design the campaigns. I was excited but also anxious, hoping that these efforts would finally bring in some clients. The campaigns went live, and all I could do was wait. The first month passed, and honestly, it felt like nothing was happening. There were a few inquiries here and there, but no solid leads or clients. I started to feel the weight of my decision, wondering if I had made the right choice in investing so much into this approach.

I couldn't help but feel frustrated. After all, I had already put so much of my time, energy, and the little money I had left into this. But Chandan, ever the optimist, kept telling me to be patient. "It takes time, trust the process," he said. Patience? It was hard to come by when I felt like my future was hanging on this. But I had no other option. I didn't have a clear backup plan, so I decided to stick it out.

Days turned into weeks, and while there were a few more inquiries, it still didn't feel like enough. I was just about to give up when things slowly started to turn around. The leads started to pick up a bit, and there was more interest. I found myself attending more meetings than before, though I was still unsure whether they would lead to actual projects. Then, after almost two months of running the campaigns, I finally got the break I had been waiting for. One of the meetings turned into a closed deal—a project was secured!

The feeling was overwhelming. I had been working non-stop, doing everything from cold calling to sending countless emails, all while watching my savings drain away. But finally, this project was a win. It was the first time I had closed a deal without the usual stress of chasing people down for hours. It felt like a huge relief, almost like I had passed some invisible test.

As the weeks passed, the momentum picked up. More inquiries turned into meetings, and eventually, some of those meetings became projects. It was still slow, but it was steady. My business was finally starting to stabilize. With the first project in hand, I felt like I could breathe a little easier. For the first time in months, I didn't have to worry about how I would pay my rent next month.

The biggest change, though, was my mindset. I had started to believe that cold calling and hoping for a break was the only way. But the campaigns had proven me wrong. I had been so focused on what wasn't working that I had failed to see the potential of digital marketing.

Looking back, I realized how much I had learned in those two months. It wasn't just about patience—it was about adjusting my approach and learning from each setback. Slowly but surely, I was building something that had the potential to grow. I still wasn't out of the woods, but the road ahead seemed a little less daunting.

With my finances stabilizing, at least for the moment, I could focus on delivering quality work for my clients instead of constantly worrying about the next bill. The relief of not having to scramble for rent money each month was huge. For the first time in a while, I felt like things were finally starting to click, and the journey, though far from easy, was moving in the right direction.

Chapter 32: The Lockdown

When things were finally starting to pick up, the unexpected happened—COVID-19 struck, and the country was put under a nationwide lockdown. The timing couldn't have been worse. It felt like I had finally started to see some light at the end of the tunnel, and then, in an instant, everything came crashing down. It was as if the rug had been pulled out from under me. After months of struggling and finding my footing, everything came to a sudden halt. Businesses everywhere were shutting down, and the world felt like it was falling apart.

Luckily, there was one silver lining in all of this: I was still a one-man army at that point. I had no employees to pay, no salaries to worry about, and no overhead costs like an office full of staff. Being a small business with just myself in the picture meant that I didn't have the additional financial pressure many bigger companies were facing. While the lockdown crippled larger companies and businesses with many employees, I only had myself to worry about, which in some strange way made things a bit more manageable. But, even with that small advantage, it didn't change the fact that I was stuck in Noida with no idea how long this would last.

Food became a challenge too. Normally, I relied on a tiffin service to deliver meals to my apartment, but with the lockdown in full force, even that service came to a halt. I had food for just two more days and then found myself stuck with nothing to eat. With the entire city shut down, there was no way for me to go out and get groceries, and no way for me to return home. No one was allowed to travel, and I was left alone, struggling to figure out what to do next.

Seeing me in such a bad state, my father couldn't just stand by. Understanding the seriousness of the situation, he reached out to the local District Magistrate (DM). My father explained the entire situation, stressing that I was stuck in Noida without access to food and with no way to return home. After hearing my father's concerns, the DM granted special permission for me to travel back to our hometown. It was a rare exception, but my father's persistence and the genuine concern he showed for my well-being worked in my favor.

To make sure I wasn't stuck waiting for a train or bus, my father sent his car to come all the way to Noida, a 400-kilometer journey, to pick me up. The relief I felt when I saw that car waiting for me was indescribable. I had been struggling with isolation and uncertainty, but now, I had a way out. I no longer had to worry about food or being stuck in a city under lockdown. The drive home was long, but the relief of heading back to safety was immense. It felt like the world outside was uncertain, but at least I was heading home where I could be taken care of.

That moment taught me something important—that even when everything seems bleak, family will always be there to pull you through.

Chapter 33: A Pause in Time

Being back home was a strange but comforting experience. For the first time in almost 10-15 years, I found myself living with my parents for an extended period. The lockdown turned out to be a strange kind of blessing in disguise. It felt like a chapter from my past had come to life again—one I hadn't experienced since I was a teenager.

Living at home again felt surreal. There was no rush to start the day; I didn't need to wake up at the crack of dawn to head out to meetings or juggle work. Instead, I woke up to the smell of freshly brewed tea and the sound of my parents' voices echoing through the house. My mother, always the enthusiastic cook, spent her days experimenting with new recipes. Some days it was a rich North Indian curry, other days it was homemade bakery treats. There were no deadlines, no pressure to finish tasks—just meals, games, and long talks about everything from family gossip to memories of my childhood.

The best part, however, was the evenings. My father, who usually worked late, was now home every day. We began playing games like Ludo and cards—traditions we had lost touch with over the years. Even though I was an adult now, there was something comforting about being part of those simple family rituals again. We didn't have the distractions of the outside world, and for once, I could just be present in the moment. We'd laugh at small things, share silly anecdotes, and even debate over the best strategies to win at Ludo.

But despite these little joys, my mind was still preoccupied with my business. The lockdown had thrown everything into uncertainty. With so much time on my hands, I started diving deep into digital marketing. I had learned early on that marketing was the key to growth, but now, with all the spare time, I could really focus on it. I spent hours each day reading articles, watching videos, and researching strategies that could help my business. I would take notes, jot down ideas, and mentally prepare for the time when the lockdown would finally be over. It was almost as if the world had paused, but I couldn't afford to.

Every morning, as I sat down at my computer, I would scroll through articles and case studies, trying to piece together a plan for when business would resume. I built strategies for social media marketing, search engine optimization (SEO), and even email campaigns. I was confident these plans would help me grow my business and reach more clients. But as the days went by, frustration started to set in. What initially seemed like a brief break from the chaos of life was now turning into a never-ending wait. The lockdown was extended from 15 days to 30 days, and then to an indefinite period. It felt like the world had come to a standstill, and my plans were slowly being buried under a growing pile of "what-ifs."

I vividly remember one evening when I was sitting at the dining table, trying to focus on a marketing video, and my mother interrupted with her latest recipe idea. She wanted to know if I was interested in trying her new experimental dish—a fusion of pasta and Indian spices. It was so unlike the usual meals I'd eaten during my busy working days, but I agreed, knowing I couldn't pass up the opportunity to try something new. As we all sat down to eat, my father, with a serious face, asked me, "So, what's your plan when this lockdown ends?" I told him about my marketing research, my ideas for new strategies, and how I was planning to market my business once I could get back to work.

Well my parents were hesitant to let me go back to Noida. They were worried about the situation and wanted me to stay home until everything was completely safe. But despite their concerns, I knew I had to return. My business was waiting, and there was only so much I could do from home. The work needed to be done in Noida, and I needed to get back to it.

I tried to reassure my parents, explaining that it was important for me to go back and resume my work. "I'll be fine," I told them. "I need to go back and focus on my business. The longer I wait, the more opportunities I might miss." I could see the worry in their eyes, but I insisted that I would take all the necessary precautions.

But still, as much as I tried to stay focused, my thoughts wandered. The uncertainty of the situation left me feeling restless. There was no clear end in sight to the lockdown. The more the lockdown was extended, the more I began to lose track of time. Days merged into weeks, and weeks into months. Each day felt like a repeat of the last. The only break in the monotony was the conversations I had with my parents and the moments of fun we shared, whether it was playing a game, trying out new recipes, or reminiscing about old family stories.

It wasn't long before the frustration of not being able to put my plans into action started to build up. I had developed so many ideas, yet I had no way to implement them. The world outside felt like it was frozen, and I was stuck in a cycle of uncertainty. All I wanted was a chance to execute the strategies I had learned, to take action and move forward with my business. The plans were there, but the waiting was driving me crazy.

Chapter 34: Return to Noida

So, as I was starting to get frustrated with the endless waiting, the news finally came—the lockdown was going to be lifted on July 1, 2020. Hearing this, I felt a burst of excitement that had been missing for months. It was finally time to get back to Noida, back to work, and, most importantly, to bring to life all the strategies and plans I'd carefully crafted during the long months at home. Without wasting a moment, I went online and booked my train tickets. My mind was already racing, planning my next moves and visualizing all the ways I would implement my new found marketing knowledge.

But my parents, understandably concerned, urged me to wait a little longer. They'd grown accustomed to having me around, and they were worried about the health risks of me traveling and resettling in Noida so soon. But I couldn't hold back anymore. I understood their worry, but I was too eager to get started again. I assured them I'd be careful, but I couldn't shake the feeling that every extra day at home was another day lost.

Seeing my determination, my father made a generous and thoughtful decision. He asked me to take his car with me to Noida. This was his main vehicle, and it was a big deal for him to part with it. He wanted me to avoid the risks of public transport. Given the situation, this was a huge relief. Public transport was still a risky option, and having my own vehicle meant I could avoid crowded trains, metros, and cabs altogether. Not only did this give me peace of mind, but it also meant I could transport my equipment easily now, sparing me the hassle of shifting it multiple times during the trip. My father's gesture was a big support, and it showed just how much he cared about my safety and my ambitions.

With the car packed up and ready, I set off on July 1. The roads were quieter than usual, which gave me time to reflect as I drove. A mix of excitement and a bit of nervousness filled the air. There was something special about returning after such a long and uncertain period. As I neared Noida, the familiar streets felt different, but I was filled with hope and purpose. I was ready to take charge of my business in a way I hadn't before.

Once back in Noida, I immediately got to work. Unpacking, organizing, and setting up everything felt strangely satisfying. It was like the start of a new chapter, armed with months of insights and plans. The strategies I'd researched were finally ready to be tested in real life. The first few weeks involved a lot of groundwork—setting up my digital marketing campaigns, updating my website, and connecting with old clients and new prospects.

Slowly but surely, my hard work started to bear fruit. The inquiries I had hoped for began to come in, and I even managed to secure a few new projects. Each small success felt like a validation of all the time and effort I had invested during the lockdown. Watching my business pick up momentum was incredibly fulfilling and rewarding, and it confirmed that my persistence and planning were worthwhile.

The lockdown, with all its challenges and frustrations, had become the turning point. It had forced me to slow down, reassess my approach, and dive deep into areas I had once overlooked. And now, here I was, watching it all come together.

Chapter 35:
The Challenges of Growth

So, now as things seemed to be working, I found myself facing two major challenges: capital shortage and the issue of clients defaulting on payments, which I had mentioned before.

Let's start with the capital shortage issue. As my production house began landing more projects, there was still a major cash flow issue. Here's what a typical project timeline looked like from a financial perspective:

Once a project was finalized, the client would clear 50% of the payment as an advance. Then, after about 5-7 days, we'd have the shoot on mutually agreed dates. After the shoot, it would take me around another 5-7 days to edit the videos. When the initial edits were done, I'd send them to the client for review, and they'd usually come back with requests for adjustments. This back-and-forth editing phase could stretch anywhere from 15-20 days. Only once the client was satisfied would they release the remaining 50% payment.

Now, here's where the problem lay: since I didn't had the funds to buy my own equipment—I had to rent it. On paper, the numbers seemed manageable, but in reality, the rentals meant that I'd have almost nothing left to reinvest or save. These rental costs ate up a large part of the project budget, often leaving me with nothing after paying them off.

On top of that, roughly 90% of clients would default on the final payment due once they received the final video. They'd come up with every excuse imaginable—ignoring calls, claiming the quality didn't meet their expectations, or suddenly finding "issues" with the video. It became a familiar cycle. I'd deliver the work, and clients would disappear or try to evade payment.

Often, I'd have to take a hit because the rental costs were so high that even the 50% advance couldn't cover it. In addition, some clients even demanded reshoots, claiming certain shots were subpar. They would promise to cover the extra expenses, but in the end, they'd refuse to pay, and I'd be forced to absorb those costs.

I quickly realized that renting equipment was a trap. Each project would break even, but I had no margin left to cover these unexpected costs. If I wanted to improve my financial position, I needed to buy my own equipment. Owning the gear would cut costs significantly, giving me flexibility and control. But buying the equipment required an upfront investment, and that was something I didn't have.

That's when I decided to turn to my father for help. He'd seen me putting in the hours and understood my struggles. After some discussions, he agreed to lend me ₹2 lakh to invest in my own equipment. This was a huge step forward. I purchased the essential tools I needed, which immediately changed the game for me. Not only did I cut out rental expenses, but I also gained a sense of security and independence. I was no longer at the mercy of rental schedules or extra charges.

For the first time in two years, I was starting to have something left over in my pocket, and that feeling of financial stability was addictive. After months of barely scraping by, I was finally seeing some results from my hard work, and I wanted to celebrate.

And celebrate, I did! This new sense of freedom led to what I now call my "ice cream phase." Every day, without fail, I'd reward myself with two plates of momos and two to three ice creams. It wasn't just about the food; it was a way of treating myself, of savoring the results of my efforts. This went on for three whole months. I had the freedom to indulge myself, and I didn't hold back.

But, as you can imagine, this indulgence came with a price. I ended up gaining 10-12 kilos. I'd start breathing heavily just from climbing stairs, and my clothes began to feel tighter by the day. I was, quite literally, carrying the weight of my success! That's when reality set in. I realized I needed to rein in my eating habits before things got out of hand.

Looking back, this phase taught me a lot—not just about managing finances but also about balancing work and lifestyle. With a renewed sense of focus, I adjusted my approach, not only to my business but also to my daily habits. The journey was just beginning, and I knew that with every new phase, there would be new lessons waiting for me.

Chapter 36: Cutting Out the Defaults

As I started finding some stability in my business, a persistent problem that had haunted me from day one still lingered: nearly 90% of clients weren't paying their final dues. Chasing these payments had become more than just a business issue—it was a constant source of stress and frustration. Every time a project ended, instead of feeling satisfied, I was left with the dread of following up, negotiating, and often being ghosted by clients who had already enjoyed the fruits of my hard work. After putting in hours of planning, shooting, and editing, this was the last thing I wanted to deal with.

Over the past two years, I had become familiar with the types of clients who tended to default. These were the clients who always wanted "just one more edit," who acted like they were doing me a favor by giving me their business, or who habitually negotiated down to the last rupee. The challenge was that I had no choice but to accept these clients back then because I needed the business. I used to accept almost every project out of necessity because, at that time, I didn't knew how to market my business properly. Without that knowledge, clients were few and far between. So, I took on any work that came my way, including projects from clients who ultimately turned out to be unreliable with payments.

But with the new marketing skills I learned during COVID, I went from scrambling to find clients to having a steady stream of quality leads. Suddenly, I wasn't just taking projects for survival—I had the freedom to be selective.

That's when I made a firm decision to say *no* to any client who seemed like they might cause payment issues. This was a bold move, and in a business where every project mattered, saying no felt risky. But I trusted my gut—two years of experience had fine-tuned my instincts. By now, I could recognize the telltale signs of potential defaulters. A client who avoided direct questions about payments, insisted on "verbal agreements," or resisted signing contracts was likely not worth the effort. If I felt even a hint of trouble ahead, I simply declined the project.

The results of this approach were almost immediate. My default rate, which had once hovered around 90%, dropped to about 40%. Cutting down bad clients alone had been a game-changer, allowing me to breathe a bit easier and focus more on quality clients.

Yet, that 40% was still a big number, and I knew I needed to bring it down further. That's when I started using watermarks on draft videos. I informed clients from the beginning that the drafts they'd see would have a watermark that I would only remove after the final payment was received. I made sure to emphasize this in all agreements and conversations. This was no longer just about trust—I wanted them to know that my work held value, and I wouldn't part with the final product until it was paid for.

This watermark policy did wonders. It wasn't just about protecting my work; it was a way of setting boundaries and communicating that my business was professional and that payment terms mattered. Clients took the watermark rule seriously, and gradually, the default rate fell even further. Within a few months, the rate had dropped from 40% to just 5%.

Finally, I had room to breathe. For the first time since starting my production house, I didn't have to constantly worry about payments after completing a project. The small pool of clients who still tried to avoid payments were easy to deal with now, as I had the upper hand. They couldn't pressure me or take advantage because they didn't have a completed, clean video in their hands.

Having stable payments coming in consistently changed everything. With fewer non-payments, I could set aside money each month, slowly building a reserve that meant I wouldn't be living project-to-project anymore. The stability allowed me to focus more on refining my work, building client relationships, and even exploring new ideas for the business without that nagging fear of going broke.

This was a turning point for my business and for me personally. Not only did I see my business growing, but I also saw my confidence building. The fear and frustration that had once controlled me were now gone. I was running my business with clear boundaries and fair terms, and I knew I could trust my instincts to protect what I had worked so hard to build.

With this new approach, I wasn't just surviving—I was thriving. I finally had both the peace of mind and the financial security to focus on the bigger picture, knowing that I'd found a way to make my business sustainable and resilient.

Chapter 37: The 3D Disaster

As things seemed to be getting better and my business was finding some footing, it didn't mean everything was sailing smoothly. There were still many hurdles I had to navigate, and the path was far from easy. Let me share one particularly challenging project that turned into a real learning experience.

One of my previous clients, for whom I had delivered a corporate film with great success, came to me with a new requirement. They needed a 3D videos. Now, I was in no way equipped to take on a 3D project. I wasn't familiar with the intricacies of 3D animation, and I had no resources for it in-house. So, naturally, I told them, "I can't do this. I'm not into 3D." But this client had been so happy with the work I had done before, and they seemed to trust me. They insisted, "Can you find someone to get this done?"

I saw the opportunity. The project was huge in terms of budget and scope—so big that it could provide me with enough financial security to keep my business running for the next 3-4 years. I couldn't afford to let it slip away. I was in a position where I could choose the clients I wanted to work with, but this one was too important to pass up.

So, I agreed. I took a 50% advance, which gave me some initial capital to work with, and began searching for freelancers who could handle the 3D animation. But little did I know that the world of freelancing could be so full of deception.

I had no idea that many freelancers in the industry were using fake portfolios—showing work that wasn't even theirs. I started working with a freelancer who seemed promising. He had a great portfolio, and I thought he was the right fit. I transferred the advance, trusting that the project was in good hands.

But when he sent me the first draft a week later, I was horrified. The work he delivered was nothing like the samples he had shown me. It was subpar, and I could tell right away that it wasn't going to meet the client's expectations. I tried to stay calm and gave him feedback, hoping it would improve, but the quality just wasn't there.

As time passed, I kept switching freelancers, hoping to find someone who could deliver what I had envisioned. I went through 6 or 7 freelancers in total, each one promising better results than the last, but I was only met with disappointment. The project deadline was getting closer, and I had nothing substantial to show for all the time and money that had been invested. I felt completely overwhelmed.

Here's the kicker: I didn't even know how to create 3D videos myself. I had no technical expertise in 3D animation. I had taken on the project with the hope of finding someone who could do it, but now, as the deadline approached, I was trapped. I had no idea how to fix the mess I was in.

In the end, I wasn't able to deliver the project as promised. The client was waiting, and I was paralyzed with fear, wondering what would happen next. I was so embarrassed by the situation, feeling like a failure in front of a client who had trusted me with such a major project. I kept imagining the worst-case scenario: what if they asked for their advance back? If they did, my company could very well face bankruptcy and I couldn't afford that.

Thankfully, the client had some other projects in the pipeline, which helped cover the advance, and I was able to salvage the situation. But that experience was a hard pill to swallow. I felt like I had let myself and my business down. The pressure of knowing I couldn't deliver on a big promise was crushing.

That was the moment I learned an invaluable lesson: Never take on a project or responsibility that you're not fully equipped to handle. It's one thing to be ambitious and take on new challenges, but it's another to take on something outside your expertise without the proper resources or knowledge to back it up. It's okay to say no or to admit when something is beyond your capabilities.

After that incident, I became much more cautious about what projects I took on. I learned to be upfront with clients about what I could and couldn't do, and to never stretch myself too thin, especially when the stakes were high.

Chapter 38: The Big Break

In 2021, one of my biggest clients reached out to me, and at first, I honestly didn't think much of it. It seemed too good to be true, and I figured they were probably just reaching out to a bunch of video production agencies. I thought they'd get in touch with the bigger, more established names who had a more polished portfolio—ones that could impress them with their high-quality work. I was just another small agency trying to find my footing.

When they asked to meet, I wasn't feeling very confident. I had doubts about whether they would even consider us for the project. We weren't as big as the others, and I knew their expectations would be high. The thought of competing with agencies that had years of experience and bigger teams made me nervous. But still, I went ahead and met them.

To my surprise, they were receptive and seemed genuinely interested in working with us. We were given the project, and I couldn't believe it at first. But even as we started shooting their videos, I was filled with anxiety. Every time I set up a shot or pressed record, a little voice inside me would wonder, *What if they don't like it?* I'd spent so much time perfecting the videos, yet I was unsure if my work would live up to their standards.

Then came the moment when I showed them the first cut of the video. I was holding my breath, waiting for feedback. What they said next completely blew me away. They loved the video. They were thrilled with how it turned out. It wasn't just a "good job" or a "thanks," but genuine appreciation for the work we had done. I had no idea how to process it—after all, they had every reason to go with a bigger agency, but they had chosen us.

That moment felt like validation. It was like a weight had been lifted off my shoulders. I not only succeeded in landing this client but had also exceeded their expectations. It was a huge turning point for me, and from that point forward, the relationship only grew stronger.

To this day, I am still working with them and have produced more than 50 videos together. It wasn't just about making videos anymore—it was about building a partnership. With each new project, I became more confident in my abilities, and the trust they placed in me gave us the motivation to push even harder.

Looking back, that project was a defining moment in my journey. It proved that hard work, persistence, and belief in yourself could open doors, even when you feel like the odds are stacked against you. It wasn't about being the biggest or most established—it was about delivering great work, and the right people noticing it.

Now, three years later, I still look back at that first call and the first meeting with disbelief. It's amazing how one project, one client, can change everything.

Chapter 39: The Corporate Betrayal

Then in 2022, a large corporate client, an electricity producer from Chhattisgarh with a turnover of about $1 billion, approached us to create a corporate film covering their ten plants. They needed it for a presentation to the Indian government, and the scale of the project was massive. This could have been a milestone in my business's journey.

The son of the company's director was handling the project, assured us that payment would be made in full once the final film was delivered. He explained that their company didn't have an advance payment policy, which I understood, but considering the scale of the project and the stature of the company, I figured it would be a one-off situation. The amount they owed us, in the grand scheme of their billion-dollar revenue, was practically peanuts. Why would such a large corporation default on payment? That thought crossed my mind as I weighed the opportunity. This was a big client, one I didn't want to lose, and so, I agreed to proceed without the usual 50% advance that we typically required for such projects.

By this point, I had hired a small team and was no longer working alone. My employees and I traveled to Chhattisgarh at our own expense to shoot the film. The shoot lasted around 8-10 days, and throughout this time, the director's son was actively involved, accompanying us to various sites. He would chat with us like old friends, sharing stories about his family and the company's history. He made us feel like we were partners in the project, not just vendors. He even joined us for meals, joked around with the team, and made it clear that he appreciated our hard work. His words were always positive, and he constantly reassured us that everything was moving in the right direction.

It felt reassuring. His warmth and familiarity created a sense of trust. I remember him saying, "You guys are doing an incredible job. I can't wait to see the final film." With every passing day, I felt more and more confident that we were in good hands, that this was a relationship built on mutual respect. We were working with a billion-dollar company, and surely, the payment would come as promised, right?

After we wrapped up the shoot, we returned and got straight to work on editing the footage. We turned the first cut around quickly, sharing it within 10 days for their review. Since they were such a big client, I didn't add any watermarks to the film. I thought to myself, *There's no way a company this established, with a team of professionals, would backtrack on a payment.* We were trusting their word and the relationship we'd built.

But that's when the problems began. Every time I followed up for feedback or changes, we were met with excuses. *"The team's busy," "We'll get back to you soon,"* and countless other delays that dragged on for months. Each follow-up seemed to fall on deaf ears. The days turned into weeks, and the weeks into months. Six months went by, and despite my best efforts, no progress was made. Still, no payment had come through. Their team stopped responding altogether, and it became painfully clear—they had no intention of paying us for the work we had completed.

The realization hit hard. I had been fooled by the charm, the camaraderie, and the promises. I had trusted this client, a billion-dollar company, to honor its word. But when push came to shove, they treated us like an expendable resource. It felt like a punch in the gut. Here we were, a small business that had poured time, energy, and resources into this project, while a corporate giant with thousands of employees and billions in revenue had decided to exploit us. The worst part was realizing how easy it was for them to discard a smaller vendor once they no longer found us useful. All those friendly interactions, the promises, the "partnerships"—they meant nothing when it came to the final payment.

This was my first real taste of the harsh side of corporate culture. It became a sobering lesson in the ruthlessness of some businesses. The truth is, as long as you're serving their needs, they'll act like your best friend. But the moment you're no longer of value, you're treated like an afterthought, a mere inconvenience. It was a brutal eye-opener.

Since that project, I've made it a strict rule to never deviate from my payment terms, no matter how big or prestigious the client may be. I learned the hard way that no amount of charm or promises can replace the importance of securing clear payment terms upfront.

The lesson was simple: **No matter how big the client, always ensure you protect your business by sticking to your terms.** And never, ever let your guard down.

Chapter 40: Building a Legacy, One Project at a Time

It has been six years now since I took the risk and started my production house. What once seemed like an impossibility is now a living, breathing reality. I still remember those early days, full of doubt and uncertainty, wondering if I had made the right choice, or if my dreams were too big for my resources. But here I am today, reflecting on a journey that has been anything but easy, yet incredibly rewarding.

Over the course of these six years, I've had the privilege of working with over 200 corporates. From small businesses to industry giants, each project has contributed to shaping my path and expanding my horizons. With every film produced and every client served, I've seen not only my work but my business grow, generating crores of revenue in the process. There were many ups and downs along the way—moments when the road ahead seemed impossible, when clients didn't pay, or when I questioned my own capabilities. But despite those hurdles, financial stability gradually became a part of the journey, making it just a little bit easier to push forward.

There was a time when I couldn't even sustain myself financially. I wasn't sure how I would make it from one month to the next. But today, my business is not only sustaining me, but it also provides employment—not to many, but at least to some—and that is something I am truly proud of. Building a business that can give others opportunities has made all the struggles worth it.

People might say, "What's so special about this? What's there to write a book about?" And while it might seem like an ordinary story to some, to me, it is anything but. It's been my journey, and there's a unique value in sharing it—the struggles, the lessons learned, the moments of fear and doubt, and the eventual triumphs that made all the hardship worth it.

Running a business is never just about making money. It's about building something from the ground up, facing challenges head-on, and evolving through it all. Six years in, and this is just the beginning. I don't know what the future holds, but I'm ready for it. The journey continues, and I'm proud to be on it.

"Your time is limited, so don't waste it living someone else's life."

— Steve Jobs

www.ingramcontent.com/pod-product-compliance
Lightning Source LLC
Chambersburg PA
CBHW031424210526
45464CB00005B/2046